Not Your
Average
Joe

Happy Joe

Not Your
Average
Joe

JOE WHITTY

TATE PUBLISHING
AND ENTERPRISES, LLC

Published by Tate Publishing & Enterprises, LLC
127 E. Trade Center Terrace | Mustang, Oklahoma 73064 USA
1.888.361.9473 | www.tatepublishing.com

Tate Publishing is committed to excellence in the publishing industry. The company reflects the philosophy established by the founders, based on Psalm 68:11,

"The Lord gave the word and great was the company of those who published it."

Book design copyright © 2012 by Tate Publishing, LLC. All rights reserved.
Cover design by Brook Breitsprecher
Interior design by Jomar Ouano

Published in the United States of America

ISBN: 978-1-62295-300-4
1. Biography & Autobiography / Personal Memoirs
2. Biography & Autobiography / Business
13.01.04

As Told to Bruce Carlson,
Marilyn Carlson, and
Tiffany Horvath

Dedication

I dedicate this book to all of the dreamers.

My advice to you is not to let anyone get in the way of those dreams.

Acknowledgments

I believe that we are on this earth to help each other. With that belief being central to my life, I must acknowledge that so many have loved me and tended to my many needs in return. Below are just a few:

The good Lord.

My parents, for the upbringing they provided. Although poor financially, they were rich in work ethics and wealthy in friends.

My wives, Sandie and Nancy, for caring for me and my needs as a husband and putting up with all of my crazy ideas and last-minute decisions! Sandie and Nancy, you were both incredible blessings to me and our children, and my life has been richer because you were both in it. I have a sneaking suspicion you are both sharing stories about me in heaven, and I wonder what kind of explanations I'm going to have to come up with when I see you both again.

My children–Larry, Julie, Tim, and Kristel; and Carolyn, Bob, Dennis, Sue, and Mike–you made the road on the journey of life worth traveling, even crammed into a motor home every weekend in your childhood when you would rather be anywhere else in the world.

My friends—I'd need another ten books to list everyone who has touched my life, but know that your friendships, support, help mentoring, sarcastic responses to my ribbing, and laughing at all my Ole' and Lena jokes have meant the world to me.

Forty years ago, I opened the very first Happy Joe's in the Village of East Davenport. That restaurant would not have been possible without the help of the following individuals and companies—whom I thank from the bottom of heart. Without these friends, none of this would have been possible:

- ❖ Bob VanVooren, friend and attorney

- ❖ Jim and Mary Castrey, friends and mentors

- ❖ Ed and Ellie Limke (who opened their house to me and my four children on many occasions)

- ❖ Denise and Sally Sissel, *Service Press Printing*

- ❖ John Donohoe, friend

- ❖ Pat Costello, friend

- ❖ Bill Burke, Burke Marketing, business partner and friend

- ❖ Davenport Bank and Trust Company

- ❖ John Bussman, Warren Cheese

- ❖ Thoms Proestler and the Thoms family

- ❖ Sharon, Mary Lou, Tom, and Jim, siblings

- ❖ Griffith Lab in Chicago

- ❖ Steve Cowherd and siblings, Matt McDowell, Kevin Kester, and Mick Mapes, my original Team Members

- ❖ Bob Wolfe, friend and mentor

Franchisees and team members—we are what we are today because of you.

My ghost writers, Bruce Carlson, Marilyn Carlson, and Tiffany Horvath, thank you for making me sound good!

Table of Contents

Happy Joe's Is Born

Happy Joe's and Community Children

Life Lessons

Foreword

*P*eople are my passion! I am driven to do what I do, be who I am, create what I create, teach what I teach, and play the way I play because of people.

If I have ever inspired, I hope it was through my care and actions for people. I write this book to share with you how I am made up and the many challenges that come with both life and business—and the entire business of life–that have allowed me to have such incredible relationships with so many people who have touched my life. I like to think I have also touched lives in turn.

Did I always succeed? No. My very first restaurant went out of business, and I found myself with a young wife and an infant to support with no source of income. Did I always trust the right people? No. My trust has been misplaced and abused and trod upon. Did I always unerringly make the best business decisions? As everyone in my family will tell you in loud, unequivocal terms: no! But my strengths–my love of people, my willingness to work hard, and my sense of humor that I continue to bring to everything I do–have always proven greater than any hardships I've experienced in life. This book is for the underdog—for the person who knows they can still live their dreams even when everyone around tells them to give it up. I write this book for the young man I was over sixty years ago— and for the young man I still believe I am today!

This book is peppered with "Whitty-isms," which are realizations I had throughout life that helped shape the man I am today. I hope some of my experiences can be related to some event in your life and that you can utilize those experiences with your passions to make a difference in the lives of the people around you.

Whitty-ism

Make the world a better place because of your presence in it!

Meet Joe Now

Meet Joe now! (August 2012)

I look much like I would imagine a typical Midwest Santa Claus looks, with rosy cheeks, a mischievous twinkle in deep-brown eyes, and wispy tufts of salt-and-pepper hair floating under my trademark straw hat.

I didn't come from money. I didn't have famous parents who backed me financially every step of my way. I didn't marry into a wealthy family, and I didn't win the lottery. I don't even have a basic college education, being unable to afford college when I was old enough to go and then being too busy to go when I was able to afford it.

I made myself and Happy Joe's Pizza & Ice Cream a household name across the Midwest through sheer hard work, determination, a sense of humor, and a strong belief in what is right and moral. My work with children who have special needs continues at many of my restaurants today, and I can still be found in the days leading up to Christmas throwing one heck of a holiday party for any child with special needs in my city and surrounding areas.

Walk into Happy Joe's in Bettendorf, Iowa, for their lunch buffet, and chances are good that you might find me there, sitting down at my favorite round table, enjoying a slice of the taco pizza I created and made famous. I will sit there for hours, talking to customers, telling jokes, and waiting for children to come by. Any child passing me will be rewarded with a wooden nickel, good for a scoop of ice cream or bowl of frozen "Joegurt," and that child will walk away standing a little taller, a little more confident in himself, and know, without a doubt, that they are a pretty special kid.

Because Happy Joe said so.

I am not only living proof of the American dream, but proof that the American dream can become a reality for any one of us.

This is my story and yours.

Introduction

*N*ever-quittin'!

Those are the words that need to start this book. Those are good words–two that will help end this book also. Those aren't very fancy words, but they'll work just fine, because I'm not a very fancy man. The wind blowing across the prairies of North Dakota, making its way east from the Rockies, is never quittin'. By the time it reaches those ice-covered, imposing Rocky Mountains in Canada, it has gone farther than most people travel in a lifetime, and it still has a long ways to go before it dies down somewhere east of the Great Lakes.

But there's nothing "dying down" about that wind while it's visiting North Dakota. There in the plains of the northern portion of the United States it is simply the land, the sky, and the wind. That never quittin' wind is democracy at its finest, treating all people and all places equally. That wind barely even notices the tucked-away little burg of Des Lacs as it roars through there.

Des Lacs is an easy town not to notice today, and it wasn't much of a town back when I was born to Lawrence and Roberta Whitty in 1937, either. Granted, at the time I was undoubtedly oblivious to anything beyond my blankets and the breeze as I lay in my baby buggy while my mother worked in the garden or participated in the church picnic. In fact, there probably wasn't much of anything that I gave much thought to then, at least nothing I can remember.

That clutch of babies, all properly parked in their buggies at the church picnic, was a clutch of question marks, each wrapped up in his little sleeper and bedclothes. Their parents, like parents everywhere the world over then and today, wondered about the new little lives they had brought into the world. What would become of them? Who would be the butcher, the baker, and the candlestick maker? Who would grow wheat or fly an airplane or even become the new Fibber McGee or Molly on the radio?

This book is in answer to those questions about the baby in the second buggy to the left of the cottonwood tree. That Whitty kid.

The life of that Whitty kid—the third child out of five–has something to teach us all. The life of that child, Lawrence Joseph Whitty, offers all of us an understanding of how the American dream works and how it can be made to work for each of us.

Whitty-ism

The life of Happy Joe could become the life of any one of you!

The Early Years

. . . .

Of course, I have no memory of those first few years. I have no memory of the scheming and plotting my parents must have had to do to get us kids raised during the tail end of the Dirty Thirties. I have no memory of the problems that had been brought to Des Lacs and the rest of America by the Great Depression.

I have no recollection of that all-important day of December 7, 1941, when the bombing of a remote island in the Pacific became the catalyst that led the United States into the World War II or the new troubles that it brought to my family. I have no recollection of knowing we were considered poor; no recollection that some people pitied us for the material things we didn't have. But I sure remember my brothers and sisters. I remember playing with them and some of the neighbor kids outside of that little town of Des Lacs, North Dakota, and I remember having a childhood filled with love and laughter and His grace.

The Whittys, back then in 1937, named their newborn Lawrence Joseph Whitty, but I've always been called just simply "Joe." Many years later, to preserve the first name I never had the chance to use, I named my firstborn son Larry.

With the early echoes of those Dakota winds ringing in my young ears, life got awfully busy for even a baby who showed up as the new one in the family. Before I was yet in school, I found myself smack in the middle of a small herd of children. Mary Lou and Tom were the big kids and Sharon and Jim were younger than me. I got what is referred to today as the much-maligned middle child status, although it wasn't until years and years later that I was told this meant I was deprived. I didn't know I was deprived then, and I tend to forget it even today.

Life was a calliope of sounds, sights, and experiences on our little one-hundred-and-twenty-acre farm five miles outside town. The birth of a third child to a couple of poor farmers back in 1937 was of little note to the much bigger world of Des Lacs and that giant of a city, Minot, fourteen miles to the east.

Of course, we kids didn't know we were poor. Mom and Dad, however, were painfully aware of it. A lot of folks would have considered us doing well since we still had our place back in those hardscrabble days of the Great Depression, unlike many of our neighbors. However, the Whitty land on Dad's side actually did get lost to the banks during the Depression. It was my mother's father who managed to hold on to his one hundred and twenty acres of what had been a larger property. Between raising virtually all the food we ate and the cash crops Dad would sell right out of the field, we made it. Barely, but we made it.

Survival of the Whitty family didn't just happen as a matter of fate or the alignment of the stars. It took a tremendous amount of work on the part of both of my parents, plus what seemed like endless chores for the kids. Let's throw in the words "never-quittin'" again. That's the way work presented itself to the Whittys, not unlike the other families in the community. And since we never knew any different, we never stopped working.

I still haven't stopped, but then again, I'm only seventy-five. I have lots of time left to stop working if I want to.

Dad was a jack-of-all-trades, playing lots of roles, but his starring ones were those of farmer, mechanic, welder, and electrician. He, in what was becoming a popular phrase, had to do what he had to do. Lots of our neighbors, for example, weren't real sure exactly what electricity was, while Dad managed to wrest part of his living out of it.

Necessity made the rules, and Mom played by them also. In addition to raising the kids, cleaning house, doing never-ending loads of laundry, making all the meals, and putting up with Dad, she also took care of the garden as well as numerous chickens and geese. In an idle hour, she'd flit around canning hundreds of jars of produce from the garden. Additionally, she had the added burden of constantly defending her reputation for being one of the best cooks in the entire Des Lacs area against all challengers, and she likely would have given any of the ladies in faraway Minot a run for their money in that department too.

The Whitty Family (Mid-1940s)

While I was on that farm, growing up and doing what seemed to be a never-ending repetition of chores and farm tasks and labor, I swore I couldn't wait to be old enough to get away from that place. A farm was nonstop work; there was always something waiting to be done. I thought I couldn't wait to be done with it all.

Later in life when my children were grown with children of their own and I had money in the bank and a thriving business model in six states, I did what I had been longing to do for almost three decades: I bought a farm. And I still work at it nonstop.

I've come full circle from where I started out on a farm to where I am today, which is on a farm. And the journey has had a lot of heartbreak and a lot of tears but so much laughter and love and friendship and fun along the way that even my darkest moments were made bearable.

Whitty-ism

Make the journey of your life one worth traveling—every moment counts!

Cheaper to Make
a New One

rowing up in the 1930s meant we were without
a lot of things we all take for granted today.
It was impossible, of course, to forget that there
was an outhouse on our place. We were pretty much
on the cutting edge of modernity with our outhouse.
Unlike the neighbors, we had a three-holer, and that
was something to be proud of. Most folks were right
pleased about having a two-holer if they were fortunate
enough, but ours was a three-holer. I knew there was
something special about us being able to have a three-
holer, although it wasn't something I would typically
brag about. You see, when you have a three-holer, you
have two regulation-sized holes in the wooden platform
and then a third, smaller one between the two big ones
for those who still have some growing to do.

A rite of passage in our family was to have attained
sufficient breadth of beam that one could graduate up
to using one of the larger holes. And, of course, the
nature of kids is to always be pushing the envelope in
an effort to grow up in a hurry. It is entirely possible I

did my share of that myself, although I may continue to heartily deny it.

However, there in that outhouse, I should have been a bit more careful about my envelope pushing. I recall rushing out to that little building one day and suddenly coming to the conclusion that I was getting way too big to be using that itty-bitty station there in the center, and that I should be using one of the others…just like the big folks. Yep—I was fairly confident that by the grand old age of four, I was definitely mature enough and adult enough to be considered for the adult seat. It's only too bad that I also didn't consider my actual size while I was considering my maturity.

I might well have been big enough in my mind to move up to using one of those other two, but apparently I wasn't quite big enough on the other end. My confidence in easing down on that platform quickly changed into panic and disgusted terror as I found myself slipping right on through it and down to the pit below.

Some readers might not be completely up-to-date as to how an outhouse works, and just remembering what happened puts me in no mood to explain it all. It should be sufficient to say that down there in that pit is the business end of an outhouse…a place no one should *ever* be. Ever.

And there I was.

My aunt and uncle were visiting that day, and they first heard my screams. The next thing I knew, they were pulling me up and out of that mess. Soon I was standing in the sunshine outside of that little building, and folks were having a great time making an assessment of the smelly situation that was me. The entire discussion was brought to a halt when my uncle solemnly observed that it'd probably be easier to make a new one than to clean this one up.

I wanted that whole incident out of my mind so immediately that I can't even recall when it was that I did make the leap from that middle seat to one of the larger ones. But I can still recall the stench of the bottom of that pit, and my embarrassed relief at being rescued.

Whitty-ism

I learned then and there that no one should ever be afraid to ask for help, even if the situation they are in is the most humiliating place they've ever been. There's nothing wrong about reaching out to grab a hand extended to you. Then you have a responsibility to return that favor when you can by helping out someone else who might be in a big heap of what was at the bottom of that outhouse. I try to live my life with that in mind and hope that everyone I have given a hand to when they needed it most went and helped someone else. That endless circle of helping becomes never quittin' also.

The Whitty House

That little white clapboard house that I have such fond childhood memories of was innocent of any such thing as plumbing or any real central heating. It was a three-bedroom home, with the girls and boys sharing one room in the large attic of house. My brothers and I got the left side of loft, and my sisters the right. There were nails from the roof sticking out in our bedroom, and in the winter it would get so cold that a cup of water left out would freeze solid overnight. My brother Tom and I slept together in the same bed, and we wore our long underwear all winter long with our socks on our almost frozen feet, under a big horse-hair blanket that we each sought to wrap as tightly as possible around ourselves.

Being normal farm kids, my brothers and I littered our side of that room with pictures of horses and the occasional old tractor. It wouldn't occur to us until years later that maybe the attic would look better with pictures of some girls hanging up as well, a notion my sister promptly squashed once and for all. The ladder that led to that uninsulated room in the top of the house was shared by all five of us, and it was amazing how fast we could negotiate that ladder on a cold morning with an armload of clothes. Those clothes were a whole lot more fun to slide into near the stove than upstairs. The downstairs of that tiny white house consisted of a kitchen, a living room and two small bedrooms, one of which belong to my parents and the other one used by my grandfather. I smile even today when I think of that kitchen, because when asked to describe it, I'm at a loss for words. For me, that's a pretty rare thing. But the truth of the matter is that Mom was always changing the wallpaper in the kitchen whenever she got a desire for something new. She'd never remove the old wallpaper either; she'd just layer on that next pattern over the last. Every pattern consisted of some sort of flower design, so whenever the current layer started to peel, we could reminisce on the different floral designs underneath it from previous years.

There was a water pump in that kitchen, and that's where we got all our water for everything from cleaning to bathing. Water would roll off our roof into a cistern in the basement, and we would pump it right into the kitchen.

I still remember the day my sister pumped up a little brown mouse into the kitchen sink. Her screams scared my brothers and me so badly we almost stopped laughing at her.

But one thing we did have in that little house that many people didn't was lights. While many of our neighbors had to be content with flickering and half-hearted kerosene lamps, we were lucky enough to have electricity for lights. That electricity was compliments of a gas engine-driven generator in the basement of the house. We were dependent on that generator an awful lot, and unfortunately, our first hint that the gas tank had run dry was that the house would suddenly plunge into inky darkness.

That would mean a trip downstairs in pitch black darkness to refill the tank. After a few trips of stumbling around blind in that dark basement, it didn't take long for my father to come up with a better solution. He rigged up a switch on the wall that would start that generator up with the push of a button. Almost nothing ever transpired by the push of a button back then, but our magic button there on the wall made things happen.

Dad worked his "magic button" enchantment by means of his knowledge of electricity. He squeezed that knowledge out of *Popular Mechanics* magazines and whatever else he could lay his hands on about electricity. Unencumbered with anything like a license to actually do electrical work, he was still known as one of the best electricians in the area. Back then, a person could do his own electrical work but was not allowed to hire out unless he had a license. Well, licenses and electrical testing cost money back then too, and money was definitely something a struggling farmer's family didn't have.

However, our neighbors knew Dad understood this new-fangled electricity thing, and that he was a lot cheaper than a licensed electrician would be. So friends and neighbors would hire Dad, and he'd do their electrical work, leaving the customers to claim that they had done it when they got inspected. This situation left the local inspector amazed at how wonderful the local folks were at wiring their own houses and barns. Occasionally, however, that inspector would show up while Dad and I were doing the wiring work for a house that would later have to claim they did it themselves. When that would happen, we'd hide until the man left again. Dad had me climbing poles for him, and when that inspector's car came into sight, I could come down a pole almost as fast as I could make it down that bedroom ladder on a cold December morning at home.

Whitty-ism

Never be afraid to learn new things!

Spinal Meningitis

....

*I*n 1805, a bit before my time, the first recorded major outbreak of spinal meningitis occurred in Geneva, Switzerland. But this dreaded disease had been around long before that. Several other meningitis outbreaks followed, with the biggest one in the United State's hitting Cleveland in 1864. Finally, in 1906, an antiserum was developed...for horses. An American scientist, who thought people might also like a cure, worked on the vaccine further, and in 1944, penicillin was discovered to be an effective treatment against some forms of the disease in humans.

This was good news for me, because in 1945 when I was eight years old, my "suddenly getting tired" and "needing a nap" turned out to be spinal meningitis. With a 90-percent mortality rate, it was not expected I would survive the awful disease that claimed the lives of so many children.

But thanks to that 1944 discovery, that brand new penicillin drug was now on the market when I came down with the dreaded sickness.

The doctor arranged for some of that wonder drug to be flown into Minot from Minneapolis when he saw how sick I was. But it was ordered late and arrived even later, and I had lapsed into a coma by the time it finally reached my hospital. My parents were told to expect to bury me within the week. In desperation, I was given enough of that new drug to treat an adult as a last ditch effort, but most people had little hope of my recovery.

Several days passed, and I was still in a coma. I was in the same Catholic hospital where I had been born, and my parents were convinced that's where I would die. Out of desperation, my dad got to a Mrs. Pearson who lived on a neighboring farm and was supposed to be a hands-on faith healer. He snuck the woman into my hospital room, past the nuns who would have had no part of such goings-on, and he left her in the room with me.

Mrs. Pearson asked everyone else to leave and spent about an hour with me in that hospital room. Upon coming out of the room, she surveyed the knot of people gathered there on my behalf and told my mother, "I think your son will be better tomorrow." That seemed like a slim reed upon which to lean all their hopes, but that's all my parents had.

Come morning, I woke up.

But I didn't just get out of bed and go home. I lay there for about a month. Mom was of the opinion that I needed lots of fruit for my recovery. She delivered eggs and cream to the grocer, and he, in turn, delivered lots of fruit to my hospital room for me.

I thought that the fruit thing was a good idea, almost as good as the theory that I needed to drink lots of malted milks and eat lots of candy in order to get my strength back. It was, of course, a relatively easy thing to talk me into drinking lots of malts and eating lots of candy bars. It got to the point where my brother Tom and my sisters were wondering what a person had to do to catch a case of that disease.

While hospital stays back then didn't run into the thousands of dollars a day, they were still expensive. Really expensive. My parents had no insurance for such eventualities and had to scramble around to take care of the hospital bill. There were no credit cards back then that could finance a long hospital stay, and if you owed someone money, you paid them back. You didn't just run up a string of bills and declare bankruptcy.

This is where our friends really stepped in. A group of neighbors took their sheep and other livestock to the stockyards to turn them into money to help us out. Dad refinanced the truck for more money. He boarded horses at no charge for the doctors, and Mom sold off a bunch of chickens, and with what seemed to be half the town chipping in, my hospital bill was whittled down to nothing in a matter of months.

As awful as the whole thing was, it had one bright side to it. When I was finally deemed healthy enough to be released, I asked my two-hundred-and-fifty pound uncle to carry me out of the hospital. I figured that he'd be strong enough that he wouldn't drop me.

Uncle Bill Green did just what I'd asked, gently carrying me from the bed that had been my home for the past several months and depositing me just as gently into my bed at home. In the process, he also healed a several-years-long rift that had developed between him and my father. From that day on, the two of them were friends again. A little boy in a hospital can change peoples' lives pretty fast.

The day I came home from the hospital, my uncle Neal planted an evergreen tree in front of our little white house. That house is gone now—but the tree is still standing. It's about twenty feet tall now, and every time I drive by it, I remember the happy moments of my childhood, and I remember how lucky I was to be able to live them.

My 'little' tree.

Whitty-ism

Never, ever, *ever* forget that life is a precious gift. Never let past fights or hatreds keep you from the people you love, because by the time you realize what you have lost, you may never find it again.

Me and Cigarettes

*T*here were lots of lessons I learned out on the farm growing up that stayed with me my entire life. It wasn't just my mom and dad that taught me lessons—all my relatives and the entire community seemed to take it for granted back then that they all had a responsibility to show children the right direction.

In fact, it was at my uncle Neal's barn, where I was taught the evils of smoking in a lesson that still makes me shudder today. It was there that I first crossed paths with a cigarette.

You see, after I was released from the hospital, I couldn't walk. My grandma Whitty was worried that I would get knocked down regularly with all the hustle and bustle in my house, so she convinced my parents to let me go home with her and Uncle Neal for awhile. So, for first month after I got out of the hospital, I lived with them on their farm.

I'd been staying with them for about two weeks and still wasn't able to walk. My family was getting mighty worried that I might never walk again, but then one morning, I just stood up. It seemed to come naturally. Of course, I hollered for my grandma to come see and also help me, because although I was standing, I still wasn't real sure about my walking ability. Well, Grandma came racing into my room and she just kind of froze and then started smiling and hugging me. Walking followed soon after that—and my whole family came over to Grandma's to watch.

Young Joe after recovering from meningitis.

Well, after I'd started walking again, I decided I was up to spending the day with my uncle Neal working on the farm, who provided me with boots and overalls just like the other farmers. I remember that I was pretty puffed up with my own importance. It was then that Uncle Neal offered me a cigarette. A cigarette! My seven-year-old self was thrilled that I could finally act like a real farmer and sit there and smoke like the other grownups. Uncle Neal lit that thing for me, and I proceeded to be a "real" farmer. For maybe two seconds.

Suddenly, out of nowhere, my entire mouth went numb. That, in turn, was closely followed by me getting sicker than a dog. When I sought refuge in the house, it didn't take Grandma but a minute to figure out what had happened. I found my numb mouth and terribly insulted stomach were nicely complemented by a world-class chewing out from Grandma.

But she wasn't done. When Uncle Neal came in, he got the same treatment…or almost the same. He didn't have the numb mouth or the sore stomach. In retrospect, however, Grandma probably should have been giving Uncle Neal a big hug instead of a chewing out. That cigarette turned out to be both the first and the last one I ever had. Even at seven, I figured anything that had that kind of effect on a person couldn't be a good thing. I never touched the darn things again, and never had any desire to do so. I remember being a teenager and seeing all my friends sneaking their cigarettes and they would offer them to me. With that lesson my seven-year-old self learned still fresh in mind even then, I was quite vocal in turning them down.

Truth be told, however, the delinquent smoker in our family was Mother.

Mother didn't want anyone to know that she was a secret smoker, so she would sneak out to the outhouse to smoke, firmly convinced none of us knew what she was doing. Mother was a woman of uncommonly good sense, but she pretty much dropped the ball on that assumption. Even the most spacious outhouse is little more than a closet-sized room…a room frequently visited throughout the day by family members, making it both a small place and a busy place where all sorts of odors linger, whether you want them to or not. Everyone knew Mom was sneaking puffs on cigarettes in that outhouse every time they went in, but we all pretended not to know.

It has always been a bit of a mystery in our family as to how Mother thought she was going to get away with keeping her cigarette smoking any kind of secret. Maybe she was depending on the smell of that smoke being sort of overwhelmed by the other odors common to such places. But mom's cigarette stench stood out from the wide variety of other outhouse flavorings, and her "secret" was never hidden from anyone with a nose and a lick of common sense. And after my worldly seven-year-old self had gotten a taste of his first cigarette, I never could understand why Mom would even want to puff away.

Whitty-ism

Don't smoke. Anything that makes you choke, go numb, and gets you sicker than a dog isn't *ever* going to be good for you.

Dinner for All

I'm pretty sure I got my urge to feed numerous people at the same time from my mother. Mother was definitely the sit-and-have-some-dinner type of housewife. If anyone was anywhere near the house at mealtime, she could be absolutely depended on to invite them to stay for the next meal.

I'm sure some of those people just *happened* to be in the right place at the right time, and that it really was a coincidence that some people were at our house come suppertime. On the other hand, I'm also fairly certain a lot of them engineered themselves an invite simply by arranging to be around the Whitty house at mealtime. Mom's cooking was rather famous, after all.

Those spur-of-the-moment meals had their high drama like almost everything else on the farm. The appearance of an oncoming cloud of dust way out at the end of our lane would provide Mother with a problem if it was someone who might be staying for dinner, because sometimes she could find herself a bit short on the makings for said dinner.

Her response to that dilemma was immediate and played a pivotal role in the welfare of those chickens scratching around out in the yard. When Mom saw an unexpected dust cloud at the far end of our long driveway approaching mealtime, she would grab up her hatchet, burst out the back door, pounce on two or three chickens, and take them to that old stump where she'd separate the chickens from the upper portions of their anatomy.

By the time the car that had started out billowing dust clouds at the end of driveway would get halfway to the house, she'd have a big pot of water heating on the stove to use to de-feather those hapless birds.

Between whipping up a salad and a dessert, she'd de-feather those chickens, clean 'em out, and have them cut up for baked chicken or fried chicken.

It is unlikely that any of those chickens out there ever fully appreciated the role that those clouds of dust on our lane would play in their lives, and how their fate was being determined by whoever happened to decide to be at the Whitty place at the right time of day.

Looking back on those dinner rituals that occurred all through my childhood, I recognize now why it is that anytime someone comes through my doors at Happy Joe's, I want them treated like the guests they are. Every time someone came out to our farm growing up, Mom treated them like royalty, fed them the best meal they'd ever had, and she made sure they left with a full stomach and a smile on their faces.

Today, that's just how I like to see our guests leave our restaurants: talking about the best pizza they ever had with great big grins on their faces. And I think it's all due to Mom showing me at a young age that anyone who makes an effort to visit you is someone pretty special—so you'd best treat them that way.

Whitty-ism

Surprise guests coming for dinner? Get Happy Joe's. It's a lot less messy that way.

Past Mistakes

....

*I*n the midst of helping Mom with the chores inside the house and Dad with the chores outside of the house, I also tried to earn a bit a spending money for myself by hiring out to neighborhood farmers who could use an extra hand come planting and harvest time. I was a pretty good expert at plowing a field in a big tractor at a young age, as well as driving trucks overflowing with seed into town. Back in those days, of course, we didn't worry a whole lot about little details like drivers' licenses.

I certainly didn't have a license when I was driving a grain truck to town laden with grain for our neighbor Allen Axness, who'd hired me one summer for some farm labor. I learned to drive as fast as I could in order to get the truck back to the field in time for the next load. For the princely sum of eight dollars a day, I was willing to hustle fast enough to get done whatever had to be done.

My eight o'clock a.m. to four o'clock p.m. stints in the truck and on the tractor plowing his fields didn't allow me a whole lot of time to do the chores and milk the cows when I'd get home late afternoon. And the natural contrary nature of milk cows made no accommodation for all the work I had already put in that day. Working from sun up to sun down also didn't leave a young man a lot of free time to go exploring the newest uncharted territory on the map of adolescent boys–adolescent girls.

Like any other kid, I did my share of really dumb things. One of the things I did back then still gnaws on me today. I had wanted to go to the fair with some friends to look at and possibly even talk to some girls, and I knew the farmer I was working for wouldn't be letting me off from my truck-driving, field-plowing job in order to go. I remember looking around his field and realizing it was going to take at least two full days to get that job done.

I knew I really wanted to go to that fair with my friends, and I took a break for a moment and stared at the gas sediment bulb in the tractor. That bulb is what allowed the contraption to run, and I remember thinking the glass looked kind of fragile. I wondered how hard a tap with a hammer it would take to shatter that bulb, and even as I was thinking that, I tapped it with my hammer.

Nothing happened. I shook my head in disgust that I was even thinking such a dumb thing and got ready to go back to work. But then some friends of mine drove by yelling at me to hurry up and meet them at the fair, and I decide to maybe tap that bulb one more time to see how fragile it really was.

Well, that gas sediment bulb up and shattered with the second gentle hammer hit, and I hid the hammer and went to Allen and told him the tractor just up and broke down.

Gas sediment bulb

Allen Axness came out to his tractor, surveyed the situation, and decided the gas sediment bulb must have broken due to the vibrations in the field. He said it was going to take him at least a full day to go to town and get another bulb and told me to just take the rest of the afternoon off. Which I promptly did. I remember going to the fair and hanging out with all my friends, but there was this cloud of guilt hanging over my head. I knew I'd done wrong just to get out of working for a day. To this day I still feel guilty over that situation. Even small-time crime can eat at a guy's conscience.

About forty years later, Allen and I continued to be friends, and what I did to him when I was a teenager still made me feel ashamed. Allen must have been around seventy when one night I up and confessed what I did to him many decades ago. I wanted to find a gas sediment bulb, wrap it up, and present it to him along with my confession, but would you believe they didn't make them anymore? I couldn't find one anywhere, so I just told him what I did.

Well, Allen thought my story was just about the most hilarious thing he'd ever heard, and from then on until he passed on to his reward, he must have told every person he met what Happy Joe did to him as a kid. I was glad I was able to offer him so much amusement about something that had been eating away at my conscience for over four decades.

One thing I've discovered since I started Happy Joe's forty years ago is that we all do dumb things when we are kids. I have gotten well over a dozen letters over the years from former employees who worked for me as teenagers and who are now adults with families of their own. These adults have sent me checks numerous times for money they admitted to stealing from the cash register at Happy Joe's when they were younger. Most of them don't tell me their names—the majority of letters are anonymous because people seem to still be embarrassed by the mistakes they made when they were younger.

However, I remember about ten years ago, I received a letter with a $200 check in it. The letter that went with the check was from a man who'd worked for me years before—and he admitted to stealing from the restaurant. His letter went on to say that he was now married and had two young boys of his own, and he just couldn't teach them right from wrong until he made right what he'd done wrong so many years before. That letter and that check had that man's address, full name, phone number and everything on it. In addition to confessing, he was letting me know everything about him!

That letter touched me more than anything had in a long time, and I still have it in my office. I wrote that young man back to assure him all was forgiven, and to let him know his boys had a wonderful role model in the form of their honest dad. That check is still with the letter too—I just can't bring myself to cash it because I think that young man paid for his crime many times over already.

Whitty-ism

It's never too late to apologize and own up to past mistakes. We all do stupid things we are ashamed of—it's not repeating them that's important and it makes one feel good knowing you did the right thing to come clean.

Gun Safety
(or How I Shot
My Mother)

....

*M*y childhood wasn't all fun and games. I was around eight when I shot my mother. I swear, it wasn't intentional.

You see, there were a lot of foxes running around Des Lacs when I was in school, and someone started offering money for fox tails. Foxes weren't well loved by the farmers, and they figured offering a bounty on their furry hides might put a stop to some of their foraging.

It certainly made us local children, always eager for some extra cash (or, in my case, *any* cash), sit up and pay attention.

I decided I was going to take the .22 rifle hanging on the kitchen wall to school with me in hopes of finding some foxes along the way and separating them from their tails. Mom had always warned me to be careful around guns, but I thought I was definitely responsible enough for a little .22. Mom had been saying for a while that she thought I was starting to get careless with the gun, and she was proven right, much to her dismay.

When I reached up and grabbed that thing off the wall, it went off.

When it went off, my mom was sitting at the supper table. She yelled at me to put the gun right back on the wall before I got into trouble with it. I nervously did so, and then turned to look at mom.

My heart almost stopped when I saw blood coming down from her knee.

"Mom!" I remember yelling. "I shot you!"

Mom stared at me for a moment like I was speaking gibberish and then looked down at her knee. She then said a word in surprise that I can't print here because children might read this book.

I had shot her in the knee as a result of my carelessness. The guilt that washed over me put the guilt I experienced from breaking that gas sediment bulb to shame. My own mother—and I had shot her.

Of course, we took Mom to the doctor right away, and he examined her carefully and announced he was not going to take the bullet out. He didn't think it was necessary and might even harm her more. So Mom spent the rest of her life with a bullet in her knee that I put there.

Mom made the most of that bullet for the rest of her life. And it was a long one. If I apologized once to her for shooting her, I did so hundreds of times. Some people just seem to take a lifelong offense to being shot. By their son.

Years later, during the occasion of my receiving an award for my Happy Joe's restaurant, people would remark to Mom about how nice it was that Joe got an award. Her typical response was, "What I'd like to do is to give him an award for shooting me in the knee!"

Mom always knew how sorry I was for that incident and how I carried the guilt from it around. Never one to let an opportunity go to waste, when I would come visit her as an adult, she would affect a limp the entire time I was there.

My sister assured me that every time, prior to my arrival, Mom was walking just fine and that she would resume walking normally as soon as I left.

Mom could even ride a motorcycle!

Whitty-ism

Don't shoot your mom. Ever.

My First Road Trip

*G*rowing up, a country boy had to take his pleasure when and where he found it. There wasn't a lot to do in the small town of Des Lacs, so my brother Tom and I pretty much tried to be a part of everything that went on around us.

There were the 4-H meetings. 4-H is an organization that is still around today—it's a youth development organization, with one of its focuses on farming. The 4-H's stand for head, heart, hands and health, and today, there are over 6 million kids involved in 4-H. Kids can be a part of 4-H from age 9 to 19.

My brother and I liked to go to their meetings. They had the advantage of being meetings where girls would show up. We weren't real sure what to do with the girls that showed up, but we understood that being in a place with girls was better than being in a place without them.

Our involvement in 4-H is what led my brother Tom and I to live for several days on milk and chili.

When we were thirteen years old, a group of about fifteen of us involved in 4-H went to Denver to show some 4-H steers. Three different farmers driving three different cars volunteered to take us farm kids to the big city so we could see what it was like. There were fifteen of us boys that went, and our drivers were nice enough to take a bit of a detour into Montana, where a local casino had folks waiting for young, green country boys with more money than good sense. I am pleased to report we didn't keep them waiting.

We thought we were pretty big stuff, partly because we had gotten picked up and hauled on that trip in a brand-new 1950 Oldsmobile. Tom and I were certain that we were on top of the world when we started that trip, and that the casinos would prove that. But we soon found we were no match for the gamblers in Montana. I may have been all of thirteen years old then, but Big Sky Country wasn't about to let a little thing like my age come between a casino and my hard-earned cash. By the time reality hit my brother and I firmly atop the head, we were down to less than ten dollars for our weeklong stay in Colorado, which had to cover three meals a day for each of us.

Not having enough to buy decent meals for our stay in Denver, we were lucky enough to chance upon a place where we could buy some milk and chili for a total of fifty cents. We had enough money left to keep us in milk and chili for the entire stay in Denver. While that may have been lucky for us, in retrospect, it probably wasn't so lucky for those who had to ride back to North Dakota with us in the car.

But I wasn't nearly done making some serious errors in Denver. Somehow I got selected to mail the letters the other fellows would write home each evening. I'd dutifully take them down to the corner box and deposit them each evening. I was firmly convinced I was making lots of moms and dads happy about finding out about what their children were doing in far-off Denver.

You wouldn't think that one country greenhorn could mess up a job like that...but I managed. I happened to be walking past that mailbox one day and for the first time was on the other side of it, opposite to what I had been accustomed to. There was a sign: "Keep Denver Clean." I chose not to bother everyone about how I had been depositing their mail in a garbage can every evening after they labored so hard getting those things written.

Whitty-ism

Don't tell everyone everything if you think it might hurt them.

Preparing the Way

....

The Merc and the Keg: My First Foray into the World of Restaurants

Joe Whitty—Senior year

I got out of high school at age eighteen, took two college entrance tests, and promptly flunked 'em both. But that was okay, because there wasn't a lot of money set aside for my continuing education anyway. One of my teachers had been mumbling something about my not being college material, and I figured she was right. Because she'd been mumbling that to me, I thought that meant I didn't need to try real hard on those tests anyway. By that time I had been working for my Uncle Neal in his gas station in Riverdale, so I jumped full time into working for him, washing cars and doing whatever else had to be done. I decided I really liked having a paycheck every few weeks, and college might interfere with that.

Since I had a gift of gab, my uncle put me up at the front register. It was about then that I bought a green and white '52 hardtop Mercury. I sometimes think I could go back through my life and live each moment through the different cars that I'd bought—but that Merc was my first. She'll always have a special place in my heart. You see, those Mercury's were hot cars and provided me with a machine to use in my races with my cousin, also the proud owner of a Mercury.

That hot Mercury opened up entirely new vistas for me. An increasingly important part of my life in those days was The Keg drive-in over in Minot. It was a happening place for anyone in my general age group, and I spent a lot of my time there. It also proved to be a great place to meet girls, which was, in my earnest opinion, one of the best things about it.

I was heartbroken when I heard that The Keg was going to be closed, and it was at this time that fate had plans for me.

Not knowing any better, I went to the owner, Rodney Lovedahl, to ask him if I could buy it.

Rodney had some embarrassing questions… questions about things like money.

Well, no, I told him I didn't have any money.

That prompted his sage advice that I should go out and borrow some. So before you could utter the words "dumb country kid," I found myself deep in debt and the owner of a restaurant in 1955 when I was a worldly eighteen years of age.

Drawing upon my vast experience as a restaurateur, (I'd been in the business for exactly twelve hours), I promoted the heck out of my restaurant. I told my friends about it, who were encouraged to tell their friends, who were encouraged to tell even more people. I made certain that some of the main people they told about The Keg were girls, which I saw as an important part of opening a new restaurant.

To everyone's surprise, mine included, The Keg took off. We had carhops on roller skates, and the jukebox would be jumping with "Wake Up, Little Suzie" and "Purple People Eater." The parking lot would be a scene every evening that would bring tears to the eyes of a car collector these days.

The restaurant business was tough. I found myself working fifteen hours a day and never got a weekend off. I would get up early to peel potatoes, and during business hours I fried hamburgers as fast as I could. I made my own root beer and sold the daylights out of it. There was a large aluminum tank in the bathroom upstairs. It was the only bathroom in the building and the only place I could mix the root beer.

The Keg Drive-In Restaurant (Painting by *Pat Costello*)

The root beer concentrate came in a big brown jug. I mixed the water, sugar, and syrup with a big wooden paddle and poured it into bottles. If anyone needed to use the bathroom, I would stand out on the balcony until they were finished. Not sure how well that would go over today, but it worked fine for all of us at the time, and no one ever complained about using the restroom while root beer marinated in the tub. While I'm fairly certain today's health inspector would probably not be impressed at my root beer making location, everyone else seemed to be just with fine with it at the time.

The restaurant was packed every weekend. That meant, of course, that while my friends were out running around and partying, I was hard at work flipping hamburgers.

After running The Keg for a while, I decided to trade my Mercury for a white '55 Ford convertible. I thought it would be fun to have a convertible, but in the excitement of buying it, I temporarily forgot that

I worked every weekend. My sister, Sharon, asked to drive it, so while I was inside working my butt off cooking hamburgers, she would drive by in my car with her friends. To give her credit, Sharon always did try to wave at me when she drove by in my car. I remember thinking, *Boy, that's a nice car. I wish I could drive it on weekends.*

I'm still wondering how a reasonably alert country boy could forget he worked every weekend.

Whitty-ism

This is when I realized that the restaurant business was going to require me to work when everyone else was hungry and having fun. I was to give up lunch, dinner, and weekends to be able work. But…what a great place to be when you want to be with people in the mood to have fun!

My Wife Sandie

*I*t was when I was working my tail off as usual at The Keg that I first met Sandie Gay.

Sandie had dark-brown hair she wore up in a loose bun, stood about five foot five with deep-brown eyes and had a personality that made everyone who knew her just love her.

To this day, when I look at my youngest daughter, Kristel, or in the eyes of my oldest daughter, Julie, I see Sandie looking back at me.

When I first met Sandie, I was young, too cool for words, and in absolutely no hurry to settle on just one girl when I could have a different date each week. I met her when a mutual friend recommended I hire her to give me some time off, and going with his glowing report, I promptly offered Sandie a job. I was at a point in my life where I strongly felt I needed more time to explore the world of the opposite sex around me, and saw hiring her as a way to achieve that.

Yet the more I was around Sandie, the more I realized she was something special. So, knowing what a popular guy I was, I graciously asked her out on a date.

I'd never had a girl turn me down before. But that's just what Sandie did, looking me in the eye and saying tartly, "I think you have enough girlfriends," then walking away.

Well, that got me to chasing after her, because I figured any girl who was smart enough to know not to date me was someone I wanted to get to know better. I had girls interested in me who thought I was some big shot entrepreneur and ladies' man. I'd never had anyone turn me down before because of the same reasons.

Sandie also worked as a lifeguard at the pool down the street, so whenever I had a chance and knew she was working, I would stroll around the pool deck in my swimsuit with my hairy chest all puffed out and hope she liked what she saw. Her steadfast ignoring of me got me so desperate that on more than one occasion I considered jumping into the pool and pretending to drown just to see if she would rescue me. I thought CPR might add a nice touch too, but when I realized I could just as easily be saved by one of the male lifeguards, I decided not to press my luck.

Well, she did eventually decide to rescue me and finally accepted one of my many pleas for a date. On our first date, I took her to a dance. It was a dance that her mom did not want her going to, as she thought Sandie was too young to go to dances.

That night, as I was finally dancing with the girl I'd been chasing after, her mom came storming into that dance, walked right out onto the floor, grabbed her, and took her home –just left me standing on the dance floor with no girl. It's kind of tough to be cool under those circumstances.

I started to realize then that this girl was something wonderful—and someone I probably needed to hang on to. My family just loved her, and my mom even told me that Sandie was the kind of girl I needed to settle down with.

About this time, my heart was in complete agreement with my mom's words, but Sandie still needed some convincing that I was the one for her.

One day I went to the jewelry store, picked out a gorgeous ring, presented it to Sandie, and asked her to marry me. She was very surprised, and so was I, when I nervously discovered her mom finally approved of both the ring and me.

Sandie Gay officially became Sandie Whitty when she and I got married on November 8, 1958.

Introducing Joe and Sandie Whitty

I bought a little house down the street from The Keg. I was about twenty years old and had never bought a house before, so I started walking around it like I would if I was buying a car.

I said to the guy, "How much do you want for it?"

He said, "Sixty-eight hundred dollars."

It was a one-bedroom house. The guy who owned it also owned a theater, and the carpeting was that thick red stuff you used to see in theaters. While I was walking around the house, I kicked the side of a door. After having bought a couple of cars, I guess I thought I had to give it a kick now and then.

I said, "I tell you what—I'll give you sixty-five hundred dollars for it!"

The seller nervously responded with, "Okay, I'll take 'er."

I wondered if maybe I should have offered a bit less. I also had the impression that the fellow was probably wondering if I was going to kick all the doors in the house.

Two years later in 1960, our first child, Larry Joe, was born in Minot.

We had gone to the hospital on New Year's Eve when Sandie was pretty certain our firstborn was getting ready to make an appearance.

It was getting close to the end of the day, and a friend of mine said, "You might get the first baby of the new year!"

I said, "Is that a big deal?"

He said, "You get free diapers, free this, free that," which I have to admit, sounded like a pretty get deal. Getting free stuff for letting nature take its course worked fine for me.

Well, by eleven that night, Larry still hadn't opted to make an appearance, and he was still hanging out in Sandie's stomach come midnight.

Finally the nurses called the doctor and told him it was time.

When he came to deliver the baby, he said to me, "What do you want me to get you, Joe, a boy or a girl?"

I told him I had been hoping for a boy.

Another guy was in the waiting room. He and his wife had been shopping, and he had to rush her to the hospital. Their baby came three minutes after midnight.

Larry decided not to come until fifteen minutes after, so we missed out on all the free stuff. He's been trying to make up for that late episode ever since by being early to pretty much everything ever since, but I still missed out on the free stuff. Then someone reminded me that I also missed a tax deduction.

I said, "With the amount of money I'm making, it won't make much difference."

Little did I realize that events were conspiring to make The Keg suddenly unprofitable.

But I had a healthy son, a beautiful wife, and nothing could upset me for long.

Whitty-ism

Embrace what you have today. You never know how much it means until it's gone.

From The Keg
to Cox Bakery

....

I ran that old drive-in restaurant for a little over two years, from 1956 to 1959. I made good money the first year, did okay the second year, but the third year two fast-food restaurants, Henry's and McDonald's, came to town. They came in with hamburger patties already made and French fries already cut, while I was still peeling potatoes and cutting my own fries. They could make and sell hamburgers and French fries much faster than I could.

People started going to them and sort of forgot about me. Well, I had a wife and a new baby and knew I needed to make a living. So as much as it saddened me, I ended up closing The Keg and took a job uptown working at Cox's Bakery.

After working at the bakery for six months, I was sent to a baking school in Minneapolis then to a second baking school. Then later, after sending me to yet another baking school, Cox's Bakery transferred me to Crookston, Minnesota, to run one of their bakeries.

Sandie and I moved into an apartment upstairs over the bakery, and I was back to working fifteen-hour days. I would go in at eleven p.m. and still be there at two p.m. the next day. I decided that fate was getting back at me for breaking that gas sediment bulb years earlier and possibly even for shooting Mom. Sandie decided to help me in the bakery, so she took cake-decorating classes.

Baker Joe

We had a lot of fun in that bakery, and some of the best memories I have of early married life were at that time. Our second and third kids, Julie and Tim, were born in Crookston. Being that Sandie worked there too, sometimes we would bring the kids down, and we would all have jobs to do.

On weekends we sold five loaves of bread for one dollar. People would come into town in trucks and buy thirty or forty loaves of bread. I would bake one hundred loaves of bread at a time. I would take the hundred loaves out of the oven, drop them on a screen to cool, and then run them through a bread slicer. Then I would wrap them in cellophane and run them through a little heater to seal them.

I loved baking bread, but it was very time consuming. It would take twenty or thirty minutes to mix the bread. The dough would have to set for one hour. Then I would punch it down. After that, it would set for another thirty-five or forty minutes before it rose up again. I punched it down again. It took from two to three hours to bake those hundred loaves of bread.

During the Christmas holiday, I would bake all day, two days in a row, so I could go back to Minot and spend time with the relatives. It was a two-hundred-and-fifty-mile drive to Minot. By the time we got there, I hadn't had any sleep, but of course every time we arrived, my brothers and cousins all would want to go out on the town. Needless to say, I was usually dumb enough to do it every trip. After getting back home to Crookston, I probably had about five total hours of sleep during every vacation. It usually took me about two weeks to recuperate from my Christmas vacation.

I look back on the hours I put in at that bakery and think, *Boy, I don't think anybody works that hard anymore.*

I never stopped! We would mix up the cake donuts, and as soon as we got those made, we would mix raised donuts. We had to do it that way to keep up with the baking. We would say, "Let's get goin' here!" We'd have the white bread coming up, then the rye bread, then the pumpernickel. About then, some lady would come in and order two loaves of raisin bread, so all of a sudden we had to make raisin bread. We had to make at least fifteen loaves of raisin bread, because that was the size of a batch. We then had to hope that we didn't have to discount the other thirteen to get rid of them.

On bitter-cold days, of which there were a lot in Minnesota, I always had a problem deciding how much bread to bake. The question was, "How many people are going to come by on a bitter-cold day and buy bread?" Usually it didn't seem to matter how cold it was. People still came out and bought their bread.

Once I finally got a good crew together at the bakery, I no longer went in at eleven p.m. Instead, I would go in at five a.m. and stay there until three or four. Still, it was a long day.

One day a guy named Clarence, who was around fifty years old and had some baking experience, came in and applied for a job. He could not hear or speak, but he was the best employee I ever had. He never forgot anything and did not get interrupted by phone calls. He was a godsend for me.

Clarence had a little bit of a problem, though—he had a hard time getting up in the morning. Usually when he went to bed, he would tie an alarm clock to his hand. When it went off, the vibration would eventually wake him up. But he still had a problem with being late because the vibrating alarm clock took a while to get his attention. So I came up with an idea. I bought a clock radio, the kind you can plug the coffee pot in. I then installed four big floodlights right over his bed, and wired everything together. When the clock radio went off, the floodlights would come on and blink on and off. That took care of his problem of getting up, and Clarence was never late again.

After I'd been with Cox Bakery for a while, they offered a contest with a two hundred dollar prize for the worker who could improve sales the most. Well, rather than go with everything that had been done before, I felt I had to create some new sales methods if my bakery was going to be the best one in town with the most improved sales.

This is where I really started to realize that thinking outside the box and away from what everyone else is doing can pay big dividends.

I had the idea that if I could deliver baked goods, I could pick up additional sales I was currently not getting and beat out the one other competitor in town. I asked the owners if I could be allowed to buy a van for the company, and admittedly, I was hoping that I would be allowed to drive it, leaving our other car free for Sandie to drive.

Cox's responded with something along the lines of, "No, we're not doing that. The next thing you know, everyone will want a van."

So I went out and bought a 52 Chevy van myself, went to the Polk county bank, and borrowed three hundred and fifty dollars to purchase it and another two hundred and fifty dollars to paint it. My payment was thirty-three dollars per month. I painted the van pink to match the bread wrapper from the bakery's packaging with Cox Bakery and had "We Deliver!" lettered on the side with our phone number.

People loved the idea and responded in droves.

My delivery plan worked so well I even had to have the janitor start running deliveries, because we couldn't keep up. I won the sales contest hands down. Later on, when I got my new job in Iowa and resigned to make the move, Cox asked to buy the van.

Whitty-ism

"No" is never an acceptable answer to an idea! Whether an idea is wildly successful or fails miserably, nothing is known until you try!

Murray's SuperValu and Mercy Hospital

*O*ne day in 1964, a bakery supply salesman came into the bakery and told me about an opening for a bakery manager at Murray's SuperValu in Davenport, Iowa. He suggested I talk to them, as he had recommended me, so I called them. They flew me to Davenport, we talked, and I took the job.

I was sad to leave Crookston, but the more I think about it, if I hadn't left, there would not have been a Happy Joe's, a Grandma Whitty's, an Iowa Machine Shed, General Store, Farmers Meat Market and General Store, or a Village Bakery. It's crazy how the good Lord works. You can tell He does a better job than we do.

I had said my good-byes to everyone at the bakery in Crookston and was getting ready to walk out the door, when in comes Clarence with his bags all packed. I asked him where he was going, and he used sign language to say he was going with me. I tried to explain to him that there was nothing said about him going along, but he insisted, so off we went to Davenport,

Iowa. When we got down there, lo and behold, someone else in their bakery had quit, so they hired Clarence too. Once again, the man was a godsend for me.

I'd been at Super Valu for about three years when the Catholic nuns at Mercy Hospital in Davenport talked me into opening a bakery in the hospital. That little hospital bakery is where I first started making pizza, and the nuns loved it.

One day a nun came to me and said the sales in the OB ward were down and asked me for suggestions. I said I thought we should start baking cream pies. I suggested we tell the new parents that when they have a baby at Mercy Hospital, they get their choice of any cream pie they wanted, and I would make it for them. They actually ran ads in the newspaper saying, "Have your baby at Mercy Hospital, and get your choice of a homemade pie made by Joe Whitty, our baker."

A couple months later, the same nun came into my office and said, "Joe, sales in the OB ward are up twenty percent."

I said, "I think it's because of the pies."

She wasn't so sure about that—I was pretty darn certain that more people were having babies just to get one of my pies. They were that good.

Whitty-ism

It never hurts to take credit for something that could be your fault.

Happy Joe's Is Born

From Shakey's to Happy Joe's

··

I had been working at the hospital bakery for about two years when a man named Gene Herwig, a Shakey's Pizza franchisee, heard I was a baker. Gene owned two Shakey's Pizza Parlors, one in Davenport, Iowa, and one in Albuquerque, New Mexico. Well, Gene's pizza dough needed a little help, and he thought I would be the perfect solution to make it better. He asked me to manage the Davenport Shakey's for him.

Pizza was something I had been thinking about for a while, ever since I'd seen how much the people at the hospital had liked the pizzas I'd created. I realized I really enjoyed making pizzas, and seemed to have knack for inventing new ones that were well received by those who ate them.

Well, Gene asked me how much money it would take for me to come to work for him, and I threw out a random number, quite a bit more than I was making at the hospital, to start negotiations.

Rather than negotiate salary, Gene's response was immediate. "When do you want to start?"

I gave two weeks' notice, and I went to work as manager of the newly opened Shakey's in Davenport, Iowa, in 1968.

I worked for Gene for about two years in Davenport, and I guess I satisfied him with what needed to be done in Davenport. That restaurant was off and running so well and had so many customers that the Shakey's Corporation asked Gene if they could buy it from him. Gene eagerly agreed to sell his Davenport Shakey's, and then he promptly offered me the same job at his Albuquerque, New Mexico, parlor. It wasn't doing nearly as well as his Davenport location, and he asked me to improve the situation there.

I had never been to New Mexico before, so Sandie and I packed up the kids—there were four of them at this point—and headed off to the American Southwest.

It was at this time, while working at Shakey's in New Mexico, that I noticed a lot of customers would leave the store after eating pizza, and one of them would say, "Let's stop and get some ice cream someplace."

That got me to thinking, *Maybe somebody should open an ice cream and pizza parlor.*

I wrote a letter to Shakey's, explaining my idea.

Their response was quick and succinct: "Thanks, but we have our own idea people."

I didn't have any money to do anything about this little idea at that time, but that idea stuck in my mind, and I found myself talking constantly about my pizza and ice cream concept. I had drawings and couldn't get the idea out of my head.

There was this ice cream shop in Albuquerque called Soda Straw, and I would go there and just think about how cool this place was. It was just a fun place where kids loved to go and hang out. They had all these different ice cream concoctions and candies and specialty sodas, and it was bright and cheerful and perfect for families.

I thought all a guy needed to do was take a pizza parlor concept and an ice cream shop concept and combine the two—have a restaurant where half of it is devoted to dinner with the family and the other half to some great frozen desserts. It would be a one-stop shop for dinner and dessert where entire families could go to relax and laugh and have a great time.

I would show Sandie the pictures and ideas, and I would tell my buddies about it while we were having a beer. I had this vision of my place being just an amazingly fun place to visit and work. I saw balloons and birthday parties and a custom fire truck and horns and a lot of noise and a ton of laughter in my vision. I even had names for the ice cream sundaes. All I needed was the money. It was 1971, and I made a pretty good year-end bonus at Shakey's. I showed the check to Sandie.

She looked me straight in the eye, and said, "You go cash that check and quit this job. We're going to do this pizza parlor thing."

I remember telling her, "We don't even have a loan, and we don't know if anybody will loan us any money."

Sandie responded with, "If we don't do it now, we never will."

So I quit my job in New Mexico, and we came back to Davenport.

All six of us packed up, shook the dust of New Mexico from our shoes, and prepared to make Iowa our permanent home. I moved my family to Davenport.

The young Whitty family

Our home on West 16th Street in Davenport was still being leased out, and we weren't sure where we would live until that lease expired. Our good friends Ed and Ellie Limke offered to let us move in with them. We accepted their offer. Their three kids and our four kids were about the same ages, so they bunked together. Sandie and I took one of their kids' rooms. Our friendship only became stronger after staying with them for a few weeks.

Ed Limke with the Whitty and Limke kids

But before moving to Davenport officially, I went to Minot, North Dakota, first to see if I could borrow some money there. Of course, the Whitty name wasn't a real big name in the banking or lending business then, and I hit all four banks in Minot and got a lot of blank looks and negative head shakes in return. Every one turned me down.

The reason I was given over and over again was that there were too many restaurants going under.

So I came back to Davenport in the Quad Cities and went to Brenton Bank, First Bank, and Northwest Bank. I got turned down by every one of them, and I never let it slow me down. I was so excited by my idea and knew it would work. I just couldn't understand why everyone else wasn't as excited as I was.

Finally, I was running out of banks when I went to Mr. V.O. Figge's Davenport Bank and Trust. There,

I talked to Loan Officer Jim Schrader, and instead of giving me a flat no, he told me he would have to talk to the rest of the bank and get back to me.

So I decided to get back to him first.

About a day later, I showed up at the bank with this big brass horn, and I honked the horn and yelled a huge and enthusiastic birthday announcement for Jim Schrader. All of the bank employees looked at me like I was crazy, but everyone came over to Jim's desk to sing "Happy Birthday" to him. They weren't sure if they should be doing that or not, but there I was, laughing and yelling and honking the horn and forcing everyone to just laugh and sing. It was a great party, made even more so by the fact that I had no idea when Jim's birthday actually was.

Finally, Bank President V.O. Figge leaned over to Jim and yelled over the noise, "Good God, get the kid a loan and get him out of here!"

Jim Schrader himself drove me to Des Moines to get the SBA loan processed. I had to fill out a lot of papers, and I'm pretty sure parts of them weren't even filled out right. I was in such a hurry to get my loan before anyone thought better of it and took it back that I just flew through the paperwork. I think the SBA guy in Des Moines ultimately decided that, as the loan was only thirty thousand dollars, it would be easier to just give me the money versus reading what I had piled up in front of him. Plus, Jim might have shared the story about what I'd done to my last hesitant loan officer with him.

So I came home from Des Moines that day with the loan to start my new and fun pizza and ice cream restaurant, and boy was I excited.

Now all I needed was a name for the place.

Whitty-ism

Don't be afraid to share your vision with the world. Sometimes you have to do more than just talk to make people see things through your eyes.

Happy Joe's Comes to Life

*T*he name Happy Joe's ultimately came from my oldest daughter, Julie.

We were trying to think of a name when we were filling out the legal documents. We came up with Silly Joe's, Funny Joe's, Poppa Joe's, all kinds of Joe's, and none of those could be trademarked.

Finally, one morning Julie came downstairs and said, "Dad, I was thinking about this last night. Why don't you just call it Happy Joe's? If you are going to have birthdays and ice cream, it's going to be a fun place."

Wow. I was taken aback for a minute at the simplicity of the name, and then I realized it was perfect.

So I told my friend, Bob Van Vooren, about it. Bob happened to be an attorney, and he said he would check to see if we could get it trademarked. Within about a week, we had reason to believe our trademark application would be approved, and it eventually was.

Over the years, several other restaurants have tried to capitalize on our recognition by naming their restaurants something similar or almost exactly the same. We would always first approach the business politely and ask that they stop using our name, but when necessary, we went to court to protect the Happy Joe's trademark.

I had invested countless years and dreams and sweat into creating Happy Joe's, and I wasn't about to let anyone simply borrow it.

So now I had a name for my new restaurant. I had the money to put into it. My next step was deciding where I was going to put Happy Joe's Pizza & Ice Cream Parlor. I looked all over Davenport for the perfect spot. Then I heard about how Smith Drugstore in the East Village of Davenport was going out of business. I wondered if the owner of the building that leased the space for the drugstore would be interested in renting it to me.

I was told, "No, they were going to sell it."

Well, I knew I didn't have enough money to buy the building, seeing as my loan was barely enough to start the restaurant. But one thing I did have was lots of friends, several of whom were almost as excited about Happy Joe's as I was.

So I happened to ask my friend, Gene Snap, if he was interested in buying a building and letting me lease it from him. I was just joking with him (kinda), when he shrugged and said, "Sure, what building do you want?"

He bought it for sixty-five thousand dollars, and he would rent it to me for eight hundred dollars a month. Gene told me if I ever wanted to buy it back from him, he would sell it at the same price he paid for it. Of course, everyone told him I probably would not last that long anyway.

The Original Happy Joe's Pizza & Ice Cream Parlor 1972

But I knew what my vision was, and I knew I could make it work. So I took the deal and paid the rent.

One year later, I knocked on Gene's door and bought the building outright.

However, prior to the success I would enjoy, I still had to build the darn thing. I didn't have any money for carpenters, so I did my own remodeling with lots of help from family and friends. I wasn't much of a carpenter, but I got the job done precisely because of everyone chipping in. Happy Joe's would have never opened were it not for my friends and my family. I still remember, one day, a bit after we opened, I was having some additional work done, and a contractor was standing there looking around.

"Who the heck put up this sheetrock?" he asked in disbelief.

I reluctantly asked him why he wanted to know.

He responded with, "They nailed it right to the cement block and didn't use any furring strips or anything." He was absolutely appalled that I let someone get away with doing that to my own restaurant.

I didn't bother the fellow by telling him that I was the one that did it.

There weren't any windows on the side of the building, but I wasn't going to let that stop it from looking like there was. So I bought molding, shutters, and mirrors and made it look like windows from the outside. I also put an old-fashioned porch on the front.

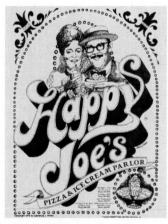

The Original Happy Joe's Pizza & Ice Cream menu (Painting by *Pat Costello*)

For the grand opening, I put the names of the businesses and people who helped me on the fake windows. I had names like the Davenport Bank and my attorney, Bob Van Vooren. Those were the days before lawyers were allowed to advertise. When Bob saw his name up there, he got extremely nervous and said he was going to get into trouble, so I took the word "Van" off the sign. I figured technically, it wasn't his name anymore so I told myself it was okay to do that.

Everyone, working side by side, did a lot of mishmash jobs to put the store together. I was using two little ovens and a used dough roller that was almost worn out and a little mixer that blew the electrical circuit every time I turned it on. I couldn't afford to buy what I really needed, but thankfully it looked good from the customers' point of view…as long as they stayed out of the kitchen.

I knew when I asked that bank for thirty thousand dollars that it was on the low side for starting up a restaurant. I hadn't decided where I was going to make up the monetary difference that it was readily becoming apparent was desperately needed.

My office desk was an old piece of Formica that I put on top of an old stove. It had a lip on the front, and that is where I would pull my chair up to. When I needed to make pasta, I took the Formica top off and cooked right there on the stove. Every time the health department inspector stopped by, the Formica top was on the stove, and they were unaware my desk doubled as a cooking station. If they had known I was using that old stove, they would have made me put in exhaust fans, and at the time, I just couldn't afford it.

I knew I wanted a soda fountain in the ice cream side of the store. A guy in Chicago remodeled used soda fountains, and because new ones were just too dang expensive, I drove down there in an old pickup to pick one up. I put a soda fountain that looked like new on the back of that old pickup, and it probably cost more than that truck did.

The day before we opened the restaurant, I called our Catholic priest, Father Hoenig. I asked him if he would hold Mass there.

He laughed when he told me, "Joe, we can't have Mass outside the church anymore, but I'll come down and bless it for you."

"Okay!" That sounded great to me.

I invited a whole bunch of our other friends to the blessing of my first store, and we had a kind of christening day for Happy Joe's. At that time, I only ever wanted or even thought about owning one restaurant that Sandie and I could run ourselves. That's all I ever hoped to have. I had no thoughts of ever franchising.

Only a few years later I had two stores open their doors in the same week in two different states. At that point I called Father Hoenig and told him he better quit praying, because I couldn't keep up with things.

But before that happened—before Happy Joe's became a fixture in the Midwest—I stood there in my very first store— and I still remember looking around just a few minutes before we opened the door for the first time.

I knew I was at the edge of a new life.

It was going to be a life where I either lost my shirt on this new adventure or a life where I fulfilled my dream of owning a successful and fun restaurant that could provide for my entire family.

I knew then, more than anything else, that I needed to have a talk with the man upstairs. So I did.

During my little conversation with Him, I promised that I'd give back to the community. I promised I'd get involved in a number of ways. And, remembering a mother with sad eyes many years ago at a Shakey's restaurant, and the hesitant smile I was able to put on the face of both her and her special little boy, I promised that one of those ways I was going to give back was by giving a party every year for children with special needs.

I've kept my promise and have been surprised to find that I've gotten as much from that as the kids have. Actually, you know what? I think I've gotten more.

Whitty-ism

Everyone has a dream. Not everyone is lucky enough to see theirs come true. Give credit to success where it is due, and always remember that with success comes responsibility. Whenever you have the opportunity to make a difference in someone's life for the better, take it! Because, ultimately, the biggest difference, you'll discover, will be in your own life.

In the News

That first week we were open, not many people came in. No one knew what Happy Joe's was or what made it so different from all the other pizza joints or ice cream stores dotting the landscapes.

And in Davenport, Iowa, in 1972, not a lot of people were very familiar with pizza or liked the pizza they had tried.

When my restaurant first opened its doors, it was unlike any restaurant anyone had ever seen. Half of it was devoted to being a pizza parlor—there was dark wood along the wall, long booths where families could scoot in together, and dark carpet along the floor. The other half of the restaurant was a brightly lit and engaging ice cream station. There were candy barrels littering the room and red and white striped pillars announcing sweet treats to one and all. It was two completely different places within the same restaurant.

But no one knew about it at the beginning. I didn't have money to hire some professional marketing team or public relations agency to come and announce my presence to the city. So here I was: I had this great, unique restaurant for families to enjoy with wonderful, delicious food—and not a single person knew anything about it!

Then one day, just a bit after we had opened, the *Time's Democrat*, which was the local newspaper and is now known as *The Quad City Times*, came down and wrote a big article about us in the East Village of Davenport. They had a picture of me behind the soda fountain and interviewed both Sandie and me. I was so excited to explain to the reporter what my vision was and what it was exactly that made Happy Joe's such a unique and fun dining experience.

That Sunday the article came out in the newspaper about my new venture. I remember I was having lunch with my family and some friends, and I had told one of my young employees, Steve Cowherd, where I would be if he needed to get a hold of me.

Well, Steve called me before I'd even had time to eat a bite and said, "You better get down here. We need some help!"

I grabbed Sandie and the four kids, hopped in our car and raced down there, only to see a line clear down to the phone booth by the street waiting to get into Happy Joe's. I stared at it in shock for a minute.

Then me, Sandie, Larry, Julie, Tim and Kristel all got to work!

It got so packed that afternoon that some people came in, ordered their pizza, and went back out to wait in their cars. Whenever a table would become vacant, I'd go out and get them. I didn't want anyone to leave without trying what I knew was the best pizza anywhere, so I started giving away free beer to people standing in line. That seemed to make a lot of people quite happy, and they were more content than ever to keep waiting.

We all worked until one that morning to get through the rush. We had a fantastic night; we ran out of dough, we ran out of pepperoni, we ran out of cheese—we ran out of almost everything. But the funny thing was, people didn't care! They were just having a great time with their family and friends at my restaurant.

It was at that point I realized that I might have something here that was lasting, could treat my family well, and that everything was going to be okay.

It was such a relief to realize that I was going to be able to work for myself instead of for somebody else.

That insane night, I could not leave the restaurant. Sandie called and asked me if I was coming home. I told her I would be home, but I just could not bring myself to leave. I wanted to be there when somebody came in. I wanted to be there to hear when someone said, "This pizza is amazing!" I wanted to be there to see their face when they ordered the big dish of ice cream, and it was expertly presented to them. I just wanted to watch people's expressions when they came in for the first time; it was just like being at a fair for me.

I used every penny of the thirty thousand dollars to open the restaurant. The day we opened, my bank account showed a zero balance.

Right around Christmas, I asked my bookkeeper, Carol Lee, how we were doing.

She said, "Joe, we have all the bills paid, and you have three hundred and fifty dollars in the bank."

I said, "I think this is going to work."

Whitty-ism

Never be afraid to reach for your dreams.

Make New Friends:
The Three Amigos

*I*t was through my brand-new Happy Joe's that I made two of the best friends of my life—men who would be with me through thick and thin. And oddly enough, our friendships came about through my determination to have the best pizza out there.

John Bussman owned the Warren Cheese Plant in Warren, Illinois. It was known he had the best cheese in the Midwest, and if you wanted mozzarella, that's where you went. Well, I needed mozzarella, and I went to John. I'd known him from my time at Shakey's Pizza in Davenport, so when Sandie and I decided to open a pizza and ice cream parlor, John was the first person I contacted for cheese and ended up being the only person I needed to contact.

This period when I opened Happy Joe's was the same time little pizza stores were popping up all over, and pizza was beginning to boom. I knew I needed to have a great product to compete with all these other places, so I knew I needed the best. To this day, my stores are required to use only the best ingredients to make the best pizzas. And, like I said before, John's place had the best cheese in the Midwest.

However, this was right about the time I was trying to make my small business loan stretch tighter than God intended it to, and quite frankly, I was almost dead broke when I called John.

I remember telling him, "John, I need your cheese for my pizzas. But I don't have any money yet."

I found out later that at the time John was getting burned by small pizza stores that were going out of business on a regular basis. All these small businesses were closing with no warning, and not one of them was paying John for the product they had bought from him and used.

John told me in surprise that there were a lot of people out there who hadn't paid him, but this was the first time somebody told him ahead of time that they couldn't pay him—even before they ordered his product. John was so surprised at my honesty he delivered the cheese, agreeing I could pay him when I had the money.

The rest is history. Happy Joe's grew almost overnight into an incredible success, and John was right there when it did. I ended up never being a day late when it came to paying him. We ended up becoming close friends as well as business associates.

The third amigo in our trio was Bill Burke.

When I opened my first Happy Joe's, Bill Burke, whose company is located in Ankeny, Iowa, was selling frozen pizza throughout the country as well as internationally.

One night while working late at my store and realizing I was low on some supplies for the next day, I saw a local sausage truck go by. I ran outside, caught up with it at the stop sign on the corner, and bought two cases of sausage on the spot.

That sausage salesman I chased down was so impressed with my game plan, and possibly my running ability, that immediately after returning to Ankeny, he suggested that his boss, Bill, contact me directly.

Well, Bill and I met, and we hit it off pretty good and he became interested in supplying not just the sausage for my pizzas, but all the meat toppings I needed. I was able to give Bill my specific recipes for all my toppings—because, if it was going to have the Happy Joe's name on it, it was going to be the best. Shortly thereafter, Bill sold off the frozen pizza business and began selling sausage and meat products for fresh pizza.

As with John Bussman and the cheese business, Bill Burke's sausage business grew with Happy Joe's pizza restaurants. At the time he began selling sausage to Happy Joe's, his business had ten employees. Today, Burke Corporation has over three hundred and fifty employees and two production facilities in Iowa and is one of the largest suppliers in the nation for meat pizza toppings.

The Burkes, the Bussmans, and my family became fast friends. Our wives enjoyed each other's company, and we went on vacations together, and our children grew up together.

Unfortunately, Bill Burke, Sr. is no longer with us, having passed away in 2010 and leaving his thriving business in the care of his son, Bill Burke Jr.

John Bussman and I still make it a point to talk regularly and catch up with each other's busy lives of children and grandchildren.

Bill, John and I were the Three Amigos in this pizza business—we all grew our fledgling business up together, and these men were with me through the happiness and tragedy that would occur throughout my life.

The Three Amigos. Happy Joe Whitty, John Bussman, and Bill Burke, Sr.

Whitty-ism

Don't be afraid to chase down people as well as your dreams. You never know who will change your life—and whose life you can also change.

The Beginning
of Franchising

*O*ne day, not long after I'd opened, an extremely nice couple from the neighboring town of Muscatine, Iowa, asked me if I'd thought about franchising. I don't think I could even spell the word at that time, but they kept bugging me. Max and Betty Brewer kept telling me they loved the concept of Happy Joe's, and they loved what I'd done with the restaurant. They said they were eager to open one in their town.

Then, not even a week after the Brewers got me thinking about the idea of franchising, a man named Al Fensterbusch came in one day and asked me if I was going to franchise. I said truthfully I didn't know if I was or not, because I hadn't thought much about it. But he sure got me to thinking even harder about it with his question.

So when Al came in and asked me a second time, I said, "I think I might."

I decided that since the Brewers had asked about it first, I needed to look into it for them. So, flying high on my recent successes in my first opening, I thought

I could sell the Happy Joe's franchise for ten thousand dollars. For a country kid like me, who still owed the bank thirty thousand dollars at the time, it seemed like the perfect win-win situation! If I put that down in my loan, I would only owe twenty thousand dollars, and I could state with pride that there were multiple Happy Joe's restaurants in Iowa. Then, thinking about Al's request to also buy one, I thought, *Well, if I could sell three of these, I would be able to pay off my loan.*

I was pretty excited about paying off my bills.

So when Max and Betty Brewer from Muscatine, Iowa, and Al Fensterbusch came and asked me about franchising again, I called my friend and counsel, Bob Van Vooren, and told him I thought I could franchise this thing. Bob admitted he didn't know anything about franchising but said he would look into it.

He called me back and said I had to get government approval to franchise, so I told him to check it out. He wanted to know what type of franchise agreements I wanted to do.

Franchise agreements?

I had no idea.

So, I'm at home thinking, *How am I going to do all this?* I knew I didn't know a thing about franchises… but then again, I also knew which restaurants *did* know a thing or two about franchising.

I went ahead and wrote letters to Dairy Queen, McDonald's and Pizza Hut, asking them if they would send me a copy of a franchise agreement. Once I got a hold of several different agreements, I went through them piece by piece. I left in what I liked, took out what I didn't, and added a bunch of items that were important to me to be a part of the foundation that Happy Joe's was being built upon.

Next, I hired a friend to type up the agreement I had just come up with, and we ended up with a seventeen-page franchise agreement.

It was shortly after that I sold my first franchise in Muscatine, Iowa, to Max and Betty Brewer.

Happy the Dog and Betty Brewer, my first franchisee

The Brewers, who didn't have a lot of money but who loved the Happy Joe's concept, and I went to their bank for a loan. Their own bank wouldn't lend them any money. So, reminded of my own loan hunting just a short while ago, we went to the other bank in town. They asked for more information, so we invited the loan officer to come to Happy Joe's in Davenport to check us out. We did the birthday party and the whole bit. He was impressed, had a great time, and agreed to loan the Brewers the money they needed. Needless to say, they promptly changed banks.

When the Brewer's opened their doors for the first time, we sent some of our young employees down to help her. Their restaurant got so busy on Saturday nights that I was always sending down people to help. They were doing great, just like we were in Davenport. I was as proud of their store as I was of mine.

Shortly after the Muscatine, Iowa, store opened, I sold Al Fensterbusch from Milan, Illinois, my second franchise. Happy Joe's was now in two states! Both stores did very well. Then I sold another Happy Joe's franchise in Cedar Rapids, Iowa; and then in Dubuque, Iowa; and then in Clinton, Iowa. After that, Happy Joe's franchises simply continued to grow like nothing I was ever able to even dream about. I was going to all of the grand openings and also running our Davenport store along with my entire family.

I remember standing in the entryway of my first restaurant and staring at my four children one day as new Happy Joe's franchises were opening every month, it seemed. Kristel, the baby, was maybe about six, and she was walking from table to table, welcoming guests and asking how they were doing. Julie, my second oldest, was busing tables, whisking plates away as soon as people were done with them. Tim, second to youngest, was standing in the kitchen on a wooden crate that allowed his short arms to reach in and do the dishes, and my oldest, Larry, wearing a straw hat, was at the front counter dishing out the most beautiful ice cream creations you ever saw.

People would come in, see them, and ask, "Are they all your kids?"

I was proud to be able say, "Yes. Yes they are."

And I was having a ball. My kids were working just as hard as anybody was, Sandie was working day and night, and we were always laughing and singing and having fun. We were living the life she and I had been dreaming of for decades—it seemed like all of our hopes for the future were coming true. I remember being so incredibly thankful for everything I had been given.

I had no way of knowing the tragedy looming over the horizon that soon would change my life, and that of my children, forever.

Whitty-ism

Involve your family in what you do. You will leave a lasting impression on them.

Tragedy Strikes

*I*t was soon after we found ourselves expanding at an incredible rate, starting franchise after franchise all over the Midwest, when everything was going too good to believe, that Sandie started feeling weak.

I remember we were in Chicago, and she was so weak she could hardly shop. I knew this wasn't like her, and I immediately became concerned.

For some reason I became convinced that her exhaustion was because her iron count was low. I simply knew that was the only reason she was so tired. I was convinced it was her iron—it was only her iron—and all she needed to do was get it checked and maybe take some pills. I refused to even consider that it could be anything else. So when we got back from Chicago, I took her to the hospital in Davenport. Then the doctor told us it wasn't her iron.

The doctor told us that we had to go to a bigger hospital in Iowa City about an hour away. While we were there, Sandie had lots of tests done on her blood.

My entire world came to a standstill when the doctors gently told us tests revealed Sandie had leukemia. Our oldest son, Larry, was all of thirteen years old. Our baby, Kristel, was barely six.

When I got home I started looking up what leukemia was all about, and I didn't find anything good about it. Sandie started treatments right away and got her white blood cell count back to where it was supposed to be. We were laughing and talking constantly about how she was going to beat this thing.

Two weeks later, Sandie went to get tested again, and her blood cell count was going out of control. She had treatment again, and this went on for about a year. Finally, it got to the point where Sandie was staying at the hospital for longer periods of time. The kids and I would go up to Iowa City and spend the whole day with her. Some days we had to wear masks and gowns and gloves, because her count was so low that it was easy for her to catch infections.

While Sandie was fighting the last battle she would ever have, our stores were jumping like crazy. My wife was in the final stages of cancer, our four children were about to lose their mother, and my business was doing better than it had ever done.

I remember desperately wishing there was some way I could switch things around. I wouldn't mind watching my business suffer if my wife could get miraculously better.

Except for maybe my bewildered youngest daughter, our children knew what was going on. They were able to go to Iowa City regularly to see their mother, although she was getting so sick they were never able to stay too long.

I knew Sandie was getting ready to leave us, and I knew I didn't want their mother's death making my children despise God. Sandie was suffering so much—and we talked about that quite a bit when we were praying for her. I started to talk to my kids about how we should pray that God would do whatever He thought would be the best for Mom rather than pray she would get better. Because I knew the chances were that Sandie wasn't going to get better.

I didn't want the kids to hate God Almighty because He didn't follow through on their prayers to heal their mom in her earthly life, so we started praying that whatever God thought was best, we would accept.

When Sandie passed away, within a year of being diagnosed with leukemia, the kids all kind of knew that was going to happen. I never tried to shield them from the reality of the situation.

When Sandie died, we had recently moved to a new house on Central Park Drive in Davenport, and I had just bought her a new car. Sandie was able to have Christmas at the house one last time, and my entire family came down to celebrate the birth of the Christ child with us. I remember that Sandie had lost all her hair and was wearing a wig. My dad was bald, and to this day I still have all the pictures of my dad wearing Sandie's wig and all of us just laughing hysterically at the resulting vision, Sandie the most of all.

My dad and mom loved Sandie. They had wanted me to marry her since the day they met her, when she would come out to the farm.

Both of our families were crushed when we lost Sandie. She was thirty-four years old when she died, and my life stopped for a while. Yet even after she was gone, I would look up when one of my daughters came into the room—maybe six-year-old Kristel or ten-year-old Julie—and from an expression on their face or a reaction to something that had happened, I would see Sandie again, even if only for a second.

It's true that we live on in our children. To this day I know Sandie hasn't gone when I listen to Kristel singing or hear Julie laugh.

My children's reactions at Sandie's funeral were a glimpse into what their adult personalities would be. Julie flitted around from person to person, trying to console everyone even as she herself needed comforting. Tim wept so hard over his mother's coffin he had to almost be pried away. Krissy was still too young to realize just how much her life had changed and stood close beside me, her large brown eyes taking in everything and everyone. And Larry, my oldest, was in such shock and trying so hard to be strong for everyone else that he just stayed in the car.

Sandie was right by my side in everything I did at Happy Joe's. She ran the soda fountain, which was not an easy job because Sandie wanted everything to be perfect. All those glasses had to be shiny. Every ice cream sundae had to be topped with whipped cream, just the right amount, not any less. Nuts had to placed and put on nicely. The cherry had to balance perfectly on the top, and the wafer had to be stuck in the side. It had to be flawless, or it didn't go out to the customer.

Sandie was behind me, supporting me and my dreams of Happy Joe's, long before they ever became a reality. She was involved in making my dreams come true from the very beginning.

I thank God she got to see how successful Happy Joe's became before she passed on, because Happy Joe's would not have existed were it not for her. And every day, I thank God for the children Sandie gave to me. She may have only been on this earth for thirty-four years, but she made more of a difference in more lives than most people who live to be one hundred do.

Whitty-ism

Cherish your time on this earth. Cherish the people who embrace it with you. And remember, even when life is at its darkest point for you, that God doesn't make mistakes.

Single Parenting

*A*fter Sandie died, I soon realized how tough it was going to be, trying to keep my business going and raising four children by myself. I didn't really know how I was going to do it.

But the company was still going, and I didn't have any choice but to jump on the train and keep it running. And I discovered that being busy offered one of the best cures for grief I've ever found. Here I was with four kids, running Happy Joe's, opening new stores, traveling all over the Midwest in a motor home, and I just took the kids with me when I could. I put them to work, and they discovered that it was okay to laugh again, it was okay to have fun, and it was okay to be a family.

They realized, and I did too, that this was exactly what their mother would have wanted for them. They would work behind the counter just like the full-time employees. Without their help, things wouldn't have been as easy for me. Without them needing me, I don't know how well I could have gone on.

When school started in the fall, I ended most of our road trips so that the kids could focus on their learning, although I knew that was going to be tough for them without their mother waiting for them when they got home from school. I was still trying to manage all my restaurants, so I wasn't able to be around as much as I would have liked.

This all came to a head one night when I came home and the house looked just like Sandie was still there. The entire place was spotless—it had been dusted and vacuumed, and toys were all put away. I didn't know what had happened, or more importantly, when it had happened.

Then twelve-year-old Julie's coach called me. Julie had quit basketball, a sport she loved that she was really good at. I was confused and worried by this, because I knew what basketball had meant to my oldest daughter.

So I asked her that night while staring around at my spotless house, "What's the deal?"

"I don't like basketball," Julie said softly.

I knew immediately that wasn't true. "Julie, what do you mean, you don't like basketball?" I asked in bewilderment.

Julie sighed and looked me straight in the eye. "Dad, I want to be here when Kristel comes home from school, and I want to be home to keep the house nice. Mom would want me to do that. Kristel needs me to do that."

I knew that wasn't true, and my heart ached for this sensitive daughter of mine, who was so busy trying to comfort everyone else she was willing to give up her own wants.

My response was immediate. "No way! Mom would want you to play basketball. How about if Dad gets somebody to come in and take care of things?"

I knew then I needed some help. I needed someone who could just be there for the children, who could listen to them when they came home from school—possibly blister their ears if they were caught doing something they shouldn't—who could hear their hopes and dreams when I wasn't around, and most importantly, I needed someone who wouldn't pity my children but help them grow up with the changes that had just changed their world.

The next Sunday, I talked with Mrs. Bernice Britt, a member of our church. I said, "Bea, are you interested in doing something?"

She said, "What do you want?"

I said, "I want somebody to be home with my kids when they come home from school. I want cookies and milk ready for them, and I want you to sit down and listen to them and talk to them about anything. I don't want you to clean the house. I don't want you to do the laundry. We'll make other arrangements for those chores. I just want you to be there when they come home."

She was a tough old cookie. I think Larry's and Tim's ears are a little longer today, because that's what she grabbed when she didn't put up with any of their crap. She was like a grandma. In fact, the kids called her Grandma Bea. She taught them how to bake cookies. And she was there for them from that day on.

I think my youngest daughter, Kristel, said it as good as anybody could. She was about eight years old and somebody said to her, "I bet you really miss your mom."

"Yup, we do," she said calmly.

"You kids are really good kids for not having a mom around."

Kristel was quiet a moment. Then she responded with, "When Mom was here, she could only watch us when she could see us. Now that she can see us all the time, we gotta be good all the time."

Sandie and I had a lot of good friends in the community who were there for us the entire time Sandie was sick and were there for the kids and me afterward. One of Sandie's dearest friends was a lady named Mary Castrey.

One day, months after Sandie had died, Mary came to me.

"Joe, it's time to get rid of Sandie's clothes," she told me firmly.

My heart sank into my stomach with the thought of going through my beloved wife's wardrobe, removing her clothes one by one from their hangers, having to fold them up, box up everything she had worn and touched, and then take it all away.

I knew it was beyond what I was capable of doing at that time.

"Mary, I just don't think I can do that," I told her hesitantly. I knew she saw the pain in my eyes. And I also knew she was right—Sandie's clothes needed to go to someone who could use them.

A few days later, knowing this huge task was before me and that it was the last thing I felt capable of doing, I came home to find Mary and Ellie Lemke, another dear friend of Sandie's, finishing up the closet cleaning.

Knowing how much it would have hurt me, these two wonderful women had waited until I was gone and then gently gone through Sandie's clothes, separating items, putting some things aside, and boxing up other items to donate.

When I came home and saw what they had done, my mouth dropped open. "What did you do?" I asked slowly

Mary looked me straight in the eyes and responded calmly, "I cleaned out your closets. Sandie won't need those clothes anymore, and they won't fit you."

Whitty-ism

Never underestimate the power of friendships. When you find a true friend, hold on tight to them.

Lessons About Franchising

*W*hen I began offering Happy Joe franchises, it seemed like everyone I knew, along with all their friends and relatives, wanted one.

Having no experience with franchising, I made a lot of mistakes in the beginning, but I believe the biggest mistake was setting up everyone I could with a franchise. I was so excited about Happy Joe's and what it had to offer, I just thought everyone else would be as well. I also thought anyone who was as excited about Happy Joe's as I was would work just as hard as I did to keep it going.

Later on I realized some people weren't any good at running a franchise because, due to their other interests, they didn't have enough time to be in the store to supervise. So they would end up hiring managers to work the stores for them so they could do other things, and they would not be in their store every day to see whatever was going on. Unfortunately, the managers they hired were not always top notch, and some of them were the exact opposite of what Happy Joe's was intended to be.

A perfect example was when I sold a franchise to two of the most reputable businessmen I knew. I trusted these men, and we were also good friends. They had solid business backgrounds and I assumed they would be perfect storeowners, being as they had so much experience behind them. Well, the problem developed when they opened a store in another state and hired someone else to manage it. As it turned out, it was precisely because they were such successful and busy businessmen that they had little time to go travel to oversee the store on any regular basis. So as a result, they had no idea what was going on in their store.

Come to find out, their manager was selling drugs out of the store. The franchise owners didn't know until the police arrested him and they got a call.

That's when I learned something extremely important about selling franchises to people. Certain people would assume they knew more about making pizzas and running a business than I did, so they tended not to listen to me and just follow their own advice. Most of these people had never run, let alone owned, a restaurant before, but they were unwilling to listen to what they needed to know, and they were also unwilling to devote the hours of work needed to make a Happy Joe's successful.

The first few people I chose to open franchises were like me. They had no money to start up, and unlike major fast-food chains, I had no financial program to help set them up. So if someone could not obtain a loan, I would take them to the bank and go into my spiel about Happy Joe's. The banker would get all excited, because I was excited, and he would give them a loan. Sometimes I would take the banker to my store on 11th Street. That usually closed the deal. I thought, back then, about President V.O. Figge instructing his loan officer to "Loan that kid the money and get him the hell out of here."

These first few franchise owners were not wealthy, but they were hard workers who knew what it took to open a restaurant and who listened to me when I told them what to continue doing to make their Happy Joe's successful. Because they didn't have a lot of money and additional business interests elsewhere, they were willing to put in the long hours necessary to learn the business, because their entire livelihood depended on making their new franchise a great place.

I would give advice to the people who needed money on how to get started. I would tell them how to approach a banker for a loan. I would tell them not to go into the bank and say, "I'm here to get a loan." They needed to say, "I picked you to be my banker." It also impressed the banker if they told him they were not going to take out much salary the first two years.

The best success stories with franchises are from the owners who listened to me, because I had been there. I had the experience. The people who do everything the way I train them are the most successful, because they learn what I learned, and they don't even have to make the mistakes I did to learn it!

And those first few franchises that I sold to individuals who needed loans and lots of hard work? Every one of them is still open today and going strong.

Whitty-ism

Not everyone is the kind of person that can make things happen. Some people are leaders, and some are followers. Some are successful because of who they work for, and some are successful because of who they are.

Iowa Machine Shed

By 1978, Happy Joe's franchises were selling better than hotcakes. I had pizza parlors springing up all over the Midwest, and the combination of pizza and ice cream was proving irresistible for our guests, who kept coming back for more.

About this time, I started thinking back on my childhood, growing up on that small farm in Des Lacs. I realized, much to my surprise, that I actually missed farming and everything it involved, despite my eager desire to get away from farming all those years ago.

Since at this point I really knew about as much about restaurants as I did about farming, I decided I really wanted to combine the two. I wanted to open a restaurant dedicated to the American farmer.

A friend of mine, Dan Whalen, owned a large building in Davenport and asked me for an idea of what to do with it. I checked it out and told him about my idea for a restaurant focused on farming with a bakery, huge cinnamon rolls, big steaks—everything needed to curb the healthy appetite of anyone who had ever spent any time out in the field.

Well, my friend thought that sounded like a fine idea, and the Iowa Machine Shed was born.

We wanted everything decorating this restaurant to be from Midwest farms—everything in the restaurant should have a purpose dealing with farming. We went to a bunch of different farms, looking for items to display in our new restaurant, asking farmers if we could take rusted and old equipment in the barns that hadn't seen the light of day since FDR was in office. Most farmers thought we were a little bit crazy, but they were all more than willing to have us tow their old and often broken items away.

I remember thinking that this restaurant needed a windmill, and so I challenged my -about to graduate from high school oldest son and general manager, Larry, in search of one. He not only found one, he was able to successfully negotiate the purchase of the windmill for the price of a steak dinner and convince some local patrons to haul it in with a crane.

When it came time to open the Iowa Machine Shed, I knew I wanted a big grand opening with everything focused on farming. So I took a big ad out in the newspaper and announced everything that was going to happen with our grand opening: we had a best-looking pig contest, a milking contest (which my mom won hands down), a tractor pull, and as it turned out, we also had lines of people waiting to get inside. We ran out of cinnamon rolls before the morning was even half over, and we ran out of pies before lunch.

I loved being a part of that—it reminded me where I came from, and it also reminded me of where I wanted to eventually end up.

Today, there are multiple Machine Sheds in the Midwest.

Dan Whalen had a son, Mike, and when Mike graduated from college, he ended up running the restaurant for us, and he did a right good job of it too. After several successful years, he asked to buy us out, and now he owns all the Iowa Machine Sheds.

Whitty-ism

If you want to be happy, try different combinations of what you love to do, and convince other people to love it to!

Dad, Meet Nancy

*R*ight in the middle of this franchise expansion and making Happy Joe's a household name in the Midwest, there I was, a single dad—and I didn't think I was making too many mistakes at it.

My daughter Julie was in high school when she discovered one of her good girlfriends also had a single parent. In this case, Julie's friend, Carolyn McGrath, had a mom raising five children solo after the death of her husband a few years earlier.

I'd never met Nancy McGrath in person before, but I had seen her outline in her doorframe several times when I would drop off her children at their house after various sporting events or school activities. All our kids were around the same age and went to school together, so it was no bother for me to take them home.

One day Julie informed me that there was a fundraising dance at her school, and that I was going. I gently tried to explain to her that it was no fun going to a dance alone. Julie then told me to take Nancy McGrath. I told my oldest daughter I'd never met the woman and that she probably wouldn't be interested in going to the dance with me.

"Dad, she's already bought a dress," Julie stated.

So I called Nancy to verify this information and laughingly told her that it was my understanding we were going to this dance together.

When I picked up Nancy, the first thing I noticed was how tiny she was. She was this petite little woman who probably weighed all of one hundred pounds. The next thing I noticed was how incredibly pretty she was. She has this chestnut-brown hair and these sparkling brown eyes, and I discovered I was more excited about going to this dance than I had originally thought.

We danced until one a.m. at Holy Family's school fundraiser. As it turned out, Nancy adored dancing. Her first husband hadn't really been into dancing, so she had a lot of lost time to make up for. We jitterbugged and waltzed and two-stepped until they threw us out.

That's when I realized I didn't want this date to end quite yet. So I did what anyone in my position would do: I asked if I could take her out for ice cream. Turned out, Nancy loved hot fudge sundaes.

Happy Joe and Nancy Whitty
at their Davenport, Iowa, farm

Of course, very few ice cream parlors are open that late at night, but I had a secret weapon: a key to Happy Joe's. I let Nancy and myself inside, and we snuck into the parlor like a couple of teenagers where I made her the best ice cream sundae she ever had. Yep—this dance thing was going mighty fine...until the police showed up.

Turns out, there was some concern about the lights being on and people sneaking into Happy Joe's long after business hours. There was some worry amongst the local law enforcement that maybe there was some hanky panky going on at Happy Joe's that night, so I was asked to come out of my own restaurant slowly with my hands in the air.

It took a minute, but after I convinced the local policemen that I was in fact breaking into my own restaurant, they decided to let me off for good behavior. Meanwhile, Nancy was watching these proceedings with her big brown eyes and a smile sneaking across her face that she was having a lot of trouble hiding.

Well, we had such a good time that night that I kind of decided maybe we should make it a permanent arrangement, and Nancy and I were married on May 8, 1976.

Then Nancy and her five children moved into our four-bedroom house. My kids, in order of appearance, were now as follows: Bob, Sue, Larry, Julie, Carolyn, Tim, Dennis, Mike, and Kristel.

Overnight, I became the father of nine children, almost all of them teenagers.

And all our lives completely changed again.

One Happy family. McGrath and Whitty
kids with Happy Joe and Nancy.

Whitty-ism

No one should ever have to endure any form of
loneliness, although one may need a hand finding their
way out of it.

Times Are a Changin'

*N*ancy was there through the boom of Happy Joe's. She was so smart and my opposite in so many good ways that made us a perfect pair. Nancy was okay with sitting in the background, so I could be forward, shaking hands, kissing babies, and opening new franchise after new franchise.

And when needed, Nancy could also move to the front. I remember being unable to attend the opening of a franchise one day due to surgery, and Nancy promptly put on my straw hat, stuck a fake moustache to her upper lip, and went to the opening, telling everyone she was me.

Our kids had to adapt to change real quick then. All our kids were around the same age, so there was some original conflict and resolution building in our house from the beginning. There was not a wallflower in our group—so you can imagine the asset I saw for Happy Joe's when my family went from five to eleven! Every one of my kids worked for Happy Joe's during at least one point in their lives, and before our first year together was over, they were all referring to each other as brother and sister. There was none of this stepbrother and stepsister talk going on—they accepted each other as siblings right away and took to bonding and fighting and making up just like brothers and sisters do.

You can probably imagine how hectic it was around the Whitty/McGrath household then, but one thing we always had was fun. Wherever we went, there was always laughter and a lot of noise.

Our motor home got a lot more crowded then too. Five people can kind of squish comfortably in a motor home as it visits Happy Joe's in multiple states, but eleven people made it a bit tighter. Since most of our kids were older, Nancy and I took to renting a room for us to sleep in when we would travel and leave the kids the motor home. It never failed that we would wake up in the morning to find three or four or five children sprawled about our room sleeping due to quarreling in the motor home, it being cooler in the hotel room, or just girls needing to get away from boys.

If I had it to do over again, the one big change I would make is buying Nancy and I a house together in the beginning. Because she sold her house and moved into my house with her kids, for a while there it was seen as "Joe's House," not "Nancy and Joe's House." I think that made it pretty tough on her. We did eventually sell that house and bought one that we could make ours together.

With that many kids now running around, you can bet I had some firm rules. Nancy and I sat down together right after we were married and made up the rules everyone in the house would be required to live by—and you can bet everyone had the same rules.

There are always growing pains with every family, and toss teenagers into the mix with those growing pains and you can imagine we didn't see eye to eye on every issue.

But those were my kids now also, and still are today. They all worked at Happy Joe's growing up, and they all knew they were the same as everyone else. I wouldn't play favorites with my children—all nine of 'em.

In fact, one time I got a call from a frustrated manager, Sid Cowherd, at one of my Happy Joe's that employed my oldest son, Larry, when he was about sixteen years old. Turns out, Larry and his new brother Bob were both working there that day, and they started horse playing, and then Larry turned the store's fire extinguisher on his brother, much to his brother's dismay. Sid wanted to know how I wanted to handle the situation.

I asked him what he would do if it was any other employee, and Sid admitted he would fire the employee. So I told him to fire Larry. In fact, I recall telling that manager if he didn't fire my son, I would fire Sid for not doing his job.

Larry lost his job that day. Larry is also now the president of Happy Joe's, so I can say that was definitely a learning experience for him that he took to heart. Sid now oversees the Happy Joe's account for our largest vendor's employ.

To this day, the whole family and their spouses and their kids and grandkids all get together for Thanksgiving and Christmas and any other occasions we can. It's always loud and always a lot of fun.

But there was only one thing about Nancy that I absolutely detested.

Nancy was this beautiful, bubbly, exciting woman whom I adored. She was an incredibly giving person who volunteered anywhere she could and just loved to help people.

But Nancy liked to smoke.

Just days before Thanksgiving of 2007, Nancy was diagnosed with lung cancer and told there was nothing the doctors could do for her.

Well, I'd already lost one wife to leukemia, and I'd be darned if I was giving this one up without a fight as well. So when the hospitals in Iowa assured me they were doing everything they could for Nancy, I didn't think it was enough. I took her to this big hospital in Texas that I'd heard was supposed to be this wonderful, miraculous cancer treatment center.

They told me they couldn't do anything more for Nancy than was already being done.

So then I decided if I wanted a miracle, I was going to ask for one where all sorts of miracles had occurred and told Nancy I was going to take her to Lourdes, France.

At this point, Nancy gently told me no more. She knew what was going to happen and knew what her smoking had caused.

The day the doctors looked at her in late May 2008 and told her she had less than a month to live, she looked at me and said, "I'm sorry."

The doctors told me to take her to hospice care for the remainder of her life. I said there was no way that was happening and picked her up right out of that hospital and took her straight home.

The hospital called me later, not real happy. I'd been in such a flustered hurry to leave, I hadn't filled out any paperwork, hadn't signed anything, and hadn't given them any additional information.

Nancy passed away on June 12, 2008, during one of the worst storms I ever remember having here in Davenport. Almost the entire family was there for her, and when the storm knocked the power out, we lit every candle we could find, surrounding the house in light.

All of Nancy's children were around her before she passed away, except for her oldest son, Bob. Bob was living out of state at the time, and he was desperately trying to catch a flight home to see his mother one last time.

The horrible storm that evening that caused the power outage also prevented Bob's flight from landing in the Quad Cities. Every few hours that evening, when we would see Nancy's eyes flicker open, we would assure her that Bob was on his way. After Bob made the heartbreaking phone call that his flight was cancelled because of the storm, we passed that news along to Nancy.

Upon hearing that, Nancy took one last breath, and then she was still.

When the funeral drivers came after Nancy had passed away, they saw all the candles we had lit leading to Nancy's bedroom, and not knowing the power had been knocked out, they thought we were having some sort of odd religious ritual.

I think Nancy smiled down from heaven at that reaction.

I did spend a little time feeling sorry for myself then. God had given me two incredible wives, and then God had taken them both away from me. It took me a little while, but I also realized that God had also given me nine children through Sandie and Nancy, and that I still had so much to be thankful for.

All those kids still call me Dad or Grandpa, and I am proud to be both.

Whittys and McGraths at the farm

We go on family vacations together and celebrate every holiday we can together.

Of the five kids I gained through marriage with Nancy, Carolyn still lives here in the Quad Cities, and she works for FedEx; Bob is in Detroit, supervising a big cleaning company there. Dennis works for a trucking company in Minnesota, and Sue is a teacher in a small town outside of Chicago. Unfortunately, Mike passed away a few years ago.

We just took a trip to Mexico together in 2011—most of my kids and grandkids and myself. There were thirty-two of us all together, and I gotta admit: I was tempted to open another franchise right there in Mexico! Because I certainly had enough people for it.

Whitty-ism

Before you argue with the man upstairs about what He has taken away from you, consider what He has given you.

Lessons Learned

....

*T*hrough these times of trial and error, one of my best friends broke my heart. It's all been forgotten, and he is still one of my best friends, but at the time I thought my world was coming apart.

My friend owned twenty-three Happy Joe's franchises and was doing quite well until he made the same mistake I had made about them: he hired a business manager to oversee his stores instead of overseeing them himself. Normally, this is the correct business step to take, but even more critical than simply hiring a business manager is making sure you hire the right business manager for the job. In this situation, the wrong person was in place, and he should have been replaced with the right person.

This was the same error I had done, hiring someone to run things and thinking they would do it just like I would. Well, this new manager considered me to be a dumb hick from North Dakota and treated me as such. He assumed, since I hadn't gone to college and didn't have a business degree, that he could outthink me and run things much better than me. He wanted to change everything about Happy Joe's that I had built up, everything that made Happy Joe's what it is, and he didn't think I was smart enough to stop him.

Let some new kid who didn't know a lick about me and where I came from take away everything my now deceased wife and I had built from the ground up with our blood, sweat, and tears?

That just wasn't going to happen.

This business manager insisted on changing ingredients for the pizzas and began buying supplies and food from unauthorized suppliers. The alternative may have offered a better pricing deal, but the quality was nowhere near what Happy Joe's stood for. He was so busy trying to save a buck that he didn't even realize the money he was saving was costing him customers. Happy Joe's was known as a place with fantastic food— and he decided he was going to change that.

He didn't understand that in any type of business there will always be someone who has a product at a better price, but if you buy by price alone, sooner or later, one way or another, you'll pay for it.

A lawsuit followed, in which my friend agreed to no longer use the name Happy Joe's. The stores in question were closed down, but soon after several of the store managers came to me, asking me to reopen their own Happy Joe's franchises. I was happy to do so.

In my evaluation of franchise applicants, I soon discovered that it is beneficial to look beyond the nature of the person interested in owning a Happy Joe's. I learned it paid dividends later on when I gave close attention to the sort of people that the person associated with, hired, and cultivated friendships with.

These were the people that would be around the new owner, and these people also needed to reflect the Happy Joe's mission.

Whitty-ism

To some extent, who we are is reflected by the kind of people we associate with.

Happy Joe's
Goes to Egypt

Happy Joe's goes to Egypt

*I*t all began in October of 1977. An Egyptian trade delegation, headed by Mohammed El Khadiga Batran, who at that time was the minister of Egypt's executive council, was visiting Bismarck, the capital of North Dakota.

The delegation was touring the United States in search of American businesses that might be interested in locating in Egypt. They had inspected numerous fast-food restaurants, such as McDonald's, but hadn't been overly impressed by anything yet. Then the governor of North Dakota took them to our Happy Joe's store for lunch.

Mr. Batran and his wife had so much fun at our Bismarck Happy Joe's and loved the pizzas so much that they rented an airplane and flew from Bismarck to the small Mount Joy airport in Iowa that week to meet me and my lawyer, Bob Van Vooren.

When Bob and I had first learned they were coming, Bob suggested I get my Happy Joe's motor home loaded up with a variety of pizza and Pepsi and that we celebrate their arrival in true Happy Joe style! So we met them at the airport carrying taco, pepperoni, and sausage pizzas and toting several liters of Pepsi with a great deal of enthusiasm.

That's when we found out they don't eat pork. And that Pepsi had been kicked out Egypt a few years earlier.

I remember laughing as I said to Bob, "Well, we sure screwed that up!"

But come to find out, the Batrans were still very enthused about Happy Joe's, and soon after our visit, they offered to fly Bob and myself to Egypt in January to talk about setting up one big pizza parlor and several franchise operations in various parts of the country. During the discussion they brought out some maps to look at for possible locations.

Well, Bob and I weren't about to turn down a free trip to Egypt, so we happily agreed and headed overseas, neither of us speaking a lick of any language other than English and rarely having ever even left the American Midwest.

So away Bob and I went to Egypt, all expenses paid. We spent the first night in the Batrans' house, and the next night they set us up in a hotel. We didn't know it was right next to a prayer tower when we first arrived. We learned that the next night. And every night after.

During the day, Bob and I would tour Cairo under the premise that we were scouting locations for the franchise. The truth was we didn't know a thing about Egypt or what would be a good location, but we sure enjoyed being tourists.

We were taken on tours of the pyramids and the sphinx. Batran had special privileges and could go anywhere. Tourists would be waiting in line while we were escorted right in through a locked gate to see the sphinx. It was a great trip.

I remember one day a gentleman offered Bob and I a free camel ride into the desert. Well, neither one of us had ever been on a camel before, but we thought, *What the heck!* and climbed on! Our happy guide took us about five miles out in the Arabian Desert and then asked us if we wanted a ride back. That's when we learned a valuable lesson: the ride into the desert was free; however, we had to pay to ride back.

As we were scouting possible locations, Bob and I kept being drawn back to the gorgeous Nile river sprawling through Cairo, and one day Bob had the idea of building Happy Joe's on a boat! When we met with the Batran's later over breakfast, Bob mentioned his boat restaurant idea, and they loved the concept.

So Bob and I spent the next three nights handwriting a contract. Between the wailing going on from the wall outside and the two of us trying to handwrite something that would make logical sense to start an Egyptian Happy Joe's franchise, I don't think either one of us slept. But when we presented the twenty-five-page contract to the Batran's, they eagerly signed it, and Bob and I headed home, while Cairo began building its first ever Happy Joe's Pizza & Ice Cream.

I originally wondered if we should change the name of the restaurant to something like "Happy جوى." But the Batrans insisted that "Joe's" would be quite appropriate, because their people loved to go to American places, and what is more American than Joe?

We spent a lot of time on long-distance phone conversations during the construction of the restaurant. I would work to get the proper equipment, blueprints, and floor plans shipped overseas to the Batrans, while they were learning all the ins and outs of the pizza business.

About six months after our original visit, it was time to open Cairo's Happy Joe's. I took a whole group of Happy Joe's friends and employees down with me for the grand opening. And it's a good thing I did.

I had a rude awakening regarding the opening of the store. I thought everything would fall into place. It didn't. The first thing that went wrong was the wiring. None of the wiring in Egypt worked with our equipment, and nothing was ready or hooked up correctly. Finally, a local man took all our equipment home with him and in three hours rewired it and brought it back. He even rebuilt a motor, and the next thing I knew, everything was working.

The next thing I saw that made me extremely nervous was the gas ovens. Normally, I have no problem cooking pizzas in gas ovens. However, when I realized the gas to heat the ovens was being siphoned into the restaurant by a simple green garden hose, I became convinced we were all going to be blown to bits.

And there was the question of how we'd fix pizza there in Egypt. We had to verify they had the right flour, ended up creating sausage for the pizza out of lamb, and I was able to introduce some new pizzas I'd created back home specifically for Egypt using chicken as the main protein.

When I asked where I could get supplies so I could show the restaurant cooks how to make a pizza, I was directed to the local market along with a twelve-year-old interpreter. Once at the bustling Cairo market, I was able to make most of my wants known. The one problem I had was when I asked for forty pounds of chicken and was handed keys to a chicken coup with around three-dozen squawking and ticked off birds inside. It took some negotiating, but eventually I was able to make the fact clear that what I needed was clean, plucked, and preferably already dead chickens made available to me.

The day before our scheduled grand opening, I cleaned the driveway. I remember sitting on the deck of that gorgeous boat in Cairo that evening, sipping a drink, and looking around. Here I was—a Midwest farm boy—getting ready to open a restaurant franchise in Egypt. I remember thinking, *I've come a long ways... I bet my mom is pretty dang proud of me right now.*

And then, just as I was silently congratulating myself on how big I'd become, a sheepherder drove a herd of sheep through the lot. And me and my big head spent the next two hours cleaning sheep dung off the parking lot. The next morning, before we were able to open, ten camels came trotting through the parking lot. So I then got the opportunity to clean camel dung. I also no longer thought about how proud my mother would be if she could see me then.

When it came to getting guests into the restaurant, I thought I needed some sort of spectacular promotion. I just wasn't sure what to do. Had I been home, I would have used my fire truck, my motorcycle, my bullhorn, and an entire list of other things at my disposal. I didn't have access to any of that stuff in Egypt.

I wish I could have had my 1948 Harley in Egypt!

Imagine my surprise when I discovered the best promotional item we could have ever had—the bathroom. We had crowds lining up to see our Happy Joe's bathroom, taking pictures of it, sometimes while people were still using it. Apparently, the novelty of having a working bathroom in this restaurant was enough to draw crowds by the hundreds. Turns out, we never had a problem getting people in the doors, and our Cairo Happy Joe's was off and running!

Altogether, between getting the restaurant ready to open and teaching new employees what goes into making Happy Joe's, I spent over a month in Cairo. I was never so happy to get home in my life.

Although that Egyptian Happy Joe's unfortunately burned down a little over a decade ago, my family still remains good friends with the Batrans. In fact, the Batrans family came down and spent Christmas 2011 with us in Davenport, Iowa, and we're now talking about opening another international Happy Joe's again.

Whitty-ism

Never be afraid to try new things! And ask your camel driver ahead of time if you have to pay to ride the camels back.

Mickey and Arthur:
A Business Model

I get asked all the time how I decide what would make a good business decision and what would not. I know my strengths, but even more important than that, I know my weaknesses.

I love to be around people. I love to laugh and to have fun and get other people as excited about my ideas as I am. I love greeting people and talking to them and telling stories and bragging about Happy Joe's. I love being a visionary. I have so many ideas on how to change things and make them better that when something occurs to me, I love to jump on it and get it done immediately. These are my strengths.

But I don't like number crunching. I don't like sitting in an office all day going over numbers and facts and figures. I don't like accounting or trying to make spreadsheets add up. I don't like being somber and serious about things I know I should be. These are my weaknesses.

I have discovered, after four decades of being in this business, that things run better if you hire people who are *not* like you.

My son Larry has always been the kind of person that asks "why" all the time. He came up with this idea of categorizing people in the work place as Mickeys or Arthurs because, at the time, his children watched a lot of kids shows and two characters named "Mickey" and "Arthur" stuck in his mind. These two distinct personalities stuck with Larry, and he came up with the idea of properly positioning people based on their attributes.

The Mickeys/Arthurs concept is based on the theory that personality type plays a huge role in the kind of position any one person should occupy. An understanding of that concept enables an employer to most effectively place people. This theory holds that basically there are two types of people: "Mickeys" and "Arthurs." This is something Happy Joe's has created to describe these two types of people and to identify where they will perform best in our restaurants.

Those who are outgoing, sensitive, popular, friendly, enthusiastic, talkative, and idealistic, to name some of their traits, are referred to as "Mickeys." In addition, "Mickeys" are idea people and dislike routine. They are concerned about their image and care about what people think of them and how they are perceived. "Mickeys" tend to be excellent hosts. They are good at making people feel welcome and appreciated. "Mickeys" will take risks and do not necessarily need all of the facts before they move forward with something. Happy

Joe's has found that the best place for "Mickeys" in our company is in the front of the house and on the floor interacting with our guests.

The second type, referred to as "Arthurs," are detail people who tend to be cautious, disciplined, analytical, complex, methodical, and precise, among other things.

Detail people like routine and want more feedback on an idea before moving forward and prefer to work within certain boundaries and rules. They insert numbers and information in order to determine if the idea should be implemented.

I am a Mickey from the top of my straw hat to the bottom of my shoes!

Happy Joe being his exuberant "Mickey" self

"Arthurs" are excellent at finding the weak link to a situation or system. Mostly, they prefer to be behind the scenes and may not enjoy the social aspect of working the floor as much as "Mickeys" do. "Arthurs" prefer dealing with facts rather than opinions and like to have as much information as possible prior to making a decision. We have found that "Arthurs" work best in the back of the house, in the production areas.

There are varying degrees of both types, and many people may carry traits of both personalities, but generally everyone will fall into one category or the other.

Neither of the two types is better than the other. They are equally important, and the key to the success of this program is that the "Mickeys" and the "Arthurs" blend their styles together in what we refer to as the "synergistic appreciation" of each other, which is required to make the system work. While the "Mickeys" are tending to the front of the house, making sure the guests are taken care of and having a good time, the "Arthurs" are in the back concentrating on production, timing, and accuracy of orders.

We at Happy Joe's have found that putting the right person in the right job makes all the difference in the world.

We've also discovered that Mickeys and Arthurs together get the best results. For example, my daughter Kristel is a Mickey and in charge of marketing for Happy Joe's. When you meet her, she's like a burst of vibrancy entering the room with enthusiasm and excitement and laughter. On the other hand, the president of Happy Joe's today is my son Larry, and he is definitely an Arthur. Larry is methodical and painstaking and reviews everything going on in the company carefully with a fine-tooth comb. He knows facts and figures and profit and loss and labor costs, and is the perfect man to have in charge of the company.

I realized early on that I needed someone very different from me to cover all the realms of possibilities in this business. I knew I needed someone who was calm and stoic, who could listen to all my grandiose schemes and ideas and politely point out what would definitely not work. I needed someone who could look at a column of numbers and tally them and realize what they meant for me and for Happy Joe's. I knew early on that for Happy Joe's to succeed, I needed an "Arthur" to balance out my "Mickey."

Larry and Kristel's personalities could not be more opposite from each other, but that is one of the reasons it works so well. Do they always get along and see eye to eye? Absolutely not. They have disagreements and conflicts and resolutions, but they both are also able to see things through the other's eyes, and having the "Mickey" and "Arthur" models helps them to both better understand why they do what they do and why the other one reacts the way they react.

Larry and Kristel together make up the perfect team: a combination of enthusiasm and professional perfectionism. I know Happy Joe's is in good hands.

Whitty-ism

To have a successful business, always recognize what your weaknesses are and seek to employ people where your weaknesses are their strengths. That way, you have all the bases covered.

Happy Joe's and
Community Children

....

Children Are Life's Most Important Assets

*I*nteracting with kids has made a lot of difference to our company since so many of those kids end up behind our counters, serving our customers.

A number of years ago, I came up with the concept of organizing fifth grade students into groups with the idea of teaching them what it will be like to be a leader. I call them "Tomorrow's Leaders." We meet once a month for the duration of a school year in the conference room at Happy Joe's headquarters in Bettendorf, Iowa.

The meetings are conducted the same as a real boardroom meeting. Two students, one boy and one girl, are selected from each of six schools in Bettendorf. I select some of the children, and others are recommended by their teachers. They need not necessarily be extra smart, but they need to be caring and eager to help others, along with having the desire to someday become leaders in the community.

I talk to them about helping other people. The idea is to do one nice thing each day for someone and make a person feel better! I emphasize that helping others gives you a nice, warm, fuzzy feeling in your tummy. Everyone must come up with an idea that will help people. The idea must be the child's own, but I give them samples like assisting handicapped children, helping elderly people, raking leaves for a stranger, etc. It's fun watching the kids as they get all excited and really have the desire to help others.

Happy Joe shaking hands with a young student

One year the group collected stuffed animals and donated them to police departments for children with family problems. The group collected so many stuffed animals that our conference room would barely hold them all. The police department sent three vans to pick them up.

Each year at our first meeting, every child must submit an idea that will help the community. These ideas are presented out loud, after which I instruct them to write down their three top choices from among those presented. At one meeting the top three were (1) send personal items to soldiers and school supplies to children in Iraq, (2) send personal items to flooding victims in Iowa, and (3) clean up a park.

Along with helping others, we discuss the dos and don'ts of living in the community as worthwhile citizens. I conduct round-table discussions on subjects such as drinking, smoking, and drugs.

In addition, I have been a member of the National Partners in Education Program since its inception in 1989. The program encourages education partnerships between the business community and the school system.

There is no limit to how a person can play an important role in the life of a child. The incidents and ideas shown above have dramatically improved the lives of children and have provided opportunities for us to benefit as a company by what we have done with children.

I may not be a trained educator, but I've picked up some techniques along the way that enable a child to see an idea they might not see otherwise. One of these is what I call my tool box idea.

I talk about how each one of us has a tool box, and how we get along in life is strongly influenced by the tools we have in our box. Using this metaphor, I teach the kids how a hammer can be like math, and a wrench is like spelling, and a screwdriver is like reading and so forth.

I explain to the kids how the bigger our tool box is, the better–and how the kind of tools we put in it can be so important. I explain how the more tools you have in your tool box, the more you will enjoy success.

I also have a bakery version of the tool box concept in which the "tools" are ingredients like salt, flour, yeast, and so forth.

I ask the kids what would happen if they were to try to make some bread and forgot to put yeast in it.

We talk about how the bread won't rise without the yeast, and it would end up being a kind of bread that no one would want to buy. I stress the importance of gathering together all the necessary ingredients while in school, all the tools they need for a successful future.

It occurred to me one day that we don't prepare our kids to get ready for some really important events like filling out a Happy Joe's application form for a job. I realized that most kids don't go through that right up until they apply for their first job. It struck me that that's a little late to practice filling out an application form.

So, I work with kids with real Happy Joe's application forms for a make-believe job. It's far better for them to make their mistakes in that sort of situation than in the reception room of a business where they want to go to work.

There is also that business of handshakes. A kid who goes to shake hands with a potential employer sure needs to have some instruction and practice in doing that little thing before the big day.

It's truly amazing how much more confident a kid can be in shaking hands if he or she has had some instruction in how to do it. It is easy for us as adults to forget how important something as simple as a good handshake is. A kid needs to go to his first job interview well armed with "social how-to skills" in that sort of thing.

Listen to any conversation among adults when they are talking about kids, and you will eventually hear about how awful it is that children cannot do something as simple as make change for a retail purchase. Listen long enough and you'll hear a horror story about how a cash register went bad in the middle of a transaction, and the kid had no idea how to calculate change.

There is nothing wrong with a cash register that calculates and displays the change owed to the customer, but a kid needs to know more than how to read the displayed amount.

I have put together talks for classes in which I explain how to make change and how important that can be. I will often go back to those classes and ask for demonstrations. My offering prizes for those who can perform the best in that area doesn't hurt a bit, of course.

And, dress! A lot of kids have no idea how to dress for an interview with someone they want to impress. A little guidance from parents can go a long way in serving the interests of a kid.

One of my favorite exercises is to get up in front of a class and tell them they are going to open a Happy Joe's store.

After lots of buzz about how they could eat pizza whenever they wanted, we get down to business.

I tell the class they need to come up with the best people in the class to handle the various jobs that have to be done in a Happy Joe's. These jobs range all the way from the dishwasher, pizza makers, and servers to the bookkeeper, and how each job is important and needs a person qualified to do that job.

I go to great lengths to explain to the kids that they need to match up jobs with people and skills and not to simply pick their best friends for one of the various positions.

We end up with the children applying for specific jobs in this mythical Happy Joe's and provide guidance to each child so he or she can convince the rest of us of their particular qualifications. It doesn't take long for the kids to focus in on what is important in terms of which kid qualifies for each position.

With a little guidance, the kids are asking the applicants not only the obvious questions about qualifications but less formal stuff like if the applicant is drug-free or not, math scores, people skills, etc.

The kids end up with a laundry list of their attributes and what makes them the perfect candidate for each job.

I have to admit my weakness is special needs children. I love those kids and never tire of working with them.

And we find they make great employees. Not only do they tend to focus very, very strongly on the task at hand, but they actually contribute to a whole different culture in the store.

I have found that when young people are around a special needs child, they will take on a different persona. They tend to act better than they would otherwise. They are far less apt to swear or to talk about inappropriate subjects.

Perhaps that is because they realize that they are likely a role model in the presence of a special needs child and act accordingly. Perhaps they know that a special child is sitting there, watching them, admiring them, and wanting to be like them.

And, oddly enough, the presence of elderly people also seems to have a similar affect on young people. Perhaps that has something to do with the fact that young people tend to behave better around their grandparents than they do around their parents.

A store with both special needs children and elderly people makes for a store where behavior problems are at a minimum.

I do hope that my interest in respect for children and my interest in their proper education aren't viewed by the readers as simply the ramblings of a soft-hearted guy who's a sucker for little people. There are really business reasons for us to concern ourselves with kids.

Whitty-ism

Our future rests in the hands of our children. Cultivate this resource, and you will leave your community, your town, and your world a better place.

All About Our Special Needs Program

....

*B*ack when I opened my first store in 1972, I certainly had no assurances that it would all work out for me. I figured the chances of seeing it all fall apart were just as good as the chances of it working out.

As I mentioned at the beginning of this book, it was those concerns that led me to ask a Catholic priest to come in and bless the restaurant. I thought that it might be a good idea to get all the positive things I could all lined up to improve the chances of Happy Joe's succeeding.

The good Father sat with me in a booth as he blessed the place, and I sat there hoping against hope that the blessing would "take."

After the priest left, I turned the lights off and again took my seat in that booth and said a little prayer.

It struck me that it might be useful to see if I could cut a little deal with the man upstairs. I told God if this restaurant worked out I'd give back to my community and to those who were in need. I told God that I'd be there for the special needs children. I couldn't help but love every single one of those kids…and I still do.

After I offered my "deal," I realized that it didn't matter if my business succeeded or not—I would still help those most in need in our society. So I sent an apology to Him for thinking I could cut a deal and decided that no matter what happened I was going to do something for children with special needs, even if my business failed and I had to go back to pumping gas.

I am driven in my work with children with special needs based on something that happened to me before I ever opened Happy Joe's. Decades earlier, while I was busy working to pull Shakey's Pizza Parlor into shape, one day a woman came in and nervously asked me if it would be okay to bring her son who was severely handicapped in to hear the piano and banjo players. Before I could even respond, she hastened to assure me that he was a good kid who would not be any trouble.

I told her of course she could bring him in. I followed that up by asking in bewilderment why she would even need to ask if she could bring her own child into what was obviously a family-friendly restaurant.

The woman was sad for a moment and revealed to me that several places had informed her they were not comfortable with her son's presence as he made the other diners nervous and uneasy due to his being handicapped. She said she always needed to ask first before she brought him in, just in case the manager didn't want him there.

Well, few things get me more upset that someone being mean to children. So I told her to bring everyone in: her whole darn family!

They came in, and I fixed this young boy up with a front-row seat to watch the musicians and did my best to make him feel special. His grandparents and other family members all came in, and everyone seemed to have a great time.

The word kind of got out that we were a place where anyone with family members or friends with special needs would be welcome and feel comfortable.

I will remember this woman and her son for the rest of my life, because I remember her sadness in revealing to me that her son was not always welcome everywhere. This was one of those events that became a turning point in my life.

Due to this event, to this day I am inspired to honor anyone with special needs. My goal has always been to make sure that anyone and everyone is welcome at all my restaurants, no matter what.

Based on what had happened almost a lifetime ago in that Shakey's restaurant, where a mother sadly informed me her child was not welcomed everywhere, I had decided that everyone was going to know they are welcome and wanted at Happy Joe's.

And that's just what I did.

It's my opinion that it is the responsibility of each one of us to help children—all children–and to ensure that they are cared for, loved, and appreciated.

From the very first year we opened, I chose one day of the year to close my restaurant to have a party for children with special needs…complete with lots of pizza, ice cream, pop, singing, dancing, Santa, and entertainment.

This is not simply a casual commitment on the part of Happy Joe's. We build it into our franchise agreements. We require our new dine-in restaurants to have a party of this type once a year.

For my first party, over forty years ago, I contacted the Truman School, which was the Special Needs School at the time. I got the principal on the phone and invited all the children over there to a Christmas party just for them at Happy Joe's.

We put a sign on the door saying the store was closed from ten a.m. to twelve p.m. for a special party—there was pizza and ice cream and Santa, and every child left there with a present.

Well, even though the sign said closed, people were still wandering in, wanting to know if they could order a pizza for lunch, and I wasn't about to turn them away. I'd say we weren't officially open, but if they wanted to stay and help, they could have a free meal. Next thing I knew, we've got strangers waiting on these kids and serving them their lunch and helping them with ice cream, and everyone is just laughing and talking and having a ball, and that's when I realized, *I gotta do this every year. And I'll need more volunteers.*

Today, four decades later, that small special needs party has evolved into a Quad-City area, two-day celebration every December. There isn't a Happy Joe's big enough to handle all the children that come now, so I rent the iWireless Center, the local stadium arena that also hosts all the local concerts and stage shows that can seat thousands. We have music and dancing and a huge celebration. There's still pizza and ice cream and Santa, and every child still leaves with a present.

Among others, there were a couple of little girls who came to the very first party forty years ago. Those little girls are all grown up now, and I look forward to seeing them each year in December.

One year the teachers introduced me to a child they said never smiled. I made it my mission to get a grin out of that boy, and he was beaming from ear to ear when he left. There was another child in a wheelchair, and he was having so much fun with the music and dancing that he crawled right out of his chair so that he could dance on the floor!

The nicest complaint I ever got was when one kid one year said, "Happy Joe, I got a complaint... I was wondering if we could make these parties last longer." Apparently a measly two hours was not nearly enough time when you are having so much fun!

I don't need any presents after that.

Two happy faces

In forty years, I've only missed one party, and that was only because my doctor absolutely refused to let me leave my hospital bed in 2003. Apparently, doctors are picky about people partying the day they have knee replacement surgery. But they took a lot of video of the party and showed it to me, and it looked like everyone had a fantastic time!

Many stores now have taken some sort of special needs party and put their own flair on it. The entire idea has just mushroomed. For example, our Kewanee store supports the Miss "You Can Do It" Pageant held for girls with special needs, and the winner gets crowned in a wonderful ceremony.

You can get an idea of what these parties are like by checking us out at www.happyjoes.com. The video from 2006 was probably one of the best. You might want to have some tissues handy before you start watching— because children can touch you more than anything else can in life.

Whitty-ism

Children are children—regardless of color, special needs, education, or background. When you make a difference in the life of a child, you have made a difference in the world.

Kids Today Are Missing Out On a Lot

I have often thought back to when I was eighteen years old and took those two college entrance tests so I could go to college.

I recall so vividly now how thoroughly I flunked those two tests–flunked 'em both. I also recall how I knew I didn't try my hardest on them, because there just wouldn't have been enough money for me to go to college anyway, even if I'd wanted to. Which I didn't really.

It was the sad results of those two tests that led me to make a full-time job out of working for my Uncle Neal in Riverdale, North Dakota. That job with Uncle Neal was the beginning of my travels through life without a college education.

I've lost lots of sleep worrying about children who encounter roadblocks in their lives. I lie awake wondering how we can let these kids know that life can go on and go on very beautifully even if they don't turn out to be "college material" or "high school material."

We have tried here at Happy Joe's to inspire kids to go on and succeed in life, finding new doors to open even as one might close up on them.

I like to think that what I have accomplished in my own life can offer encouragement to young people who might not be this "material" or that "material."

No matter what happens in life, we all have to recognize that when you make any decision, you're also giving up another decision. And you have to be okay with that, because you'll never be satisfied with the choice you have made until you don't dwell on the decision you didn't make. If you spend a lot of time thinking about what you didn't do, you're not going to be productive. Focus on the choices you have made—not the ones you haven't.

So you chose not to go college. Instead of spending the rest of your life thinking about how your life would have been different with a degree behind your name, think about the future you have now and where you want it to be.

One of my favorite recollections about a high school kid who seemed to be drifting down a dead-end street was the life of a young fellow who appeared to have a special talent for getting into trouble. He always seemed to be finding trouble of some sort during hours when he should have been in school but wasn't.

The school, authorities, and maybe even his parents had just about given up on the young man when I got introduced to him.

I told the young fellow that I'd give him a free pizza every week if he had perfect attendance at school that week.

Apparently the way to that boy's future was through his stomach. He took me up on the deal, and I found myself giving this kid a free pizza every week until he graduated from high school.

Another boy didn't have an attendance problem but simply wouldn't do the work assigned to him. He was at the edge of flunking out when I met him. He had picked up some criminal habits by that time also.

I cut a deal with the judge in which the kid would be able to stay out of the local youth detention center if I'd give him a job and help him turn his life around.

The kid and I drew up a contract outlining what he'd have to do to get and keep a job with Happy Joe's as an alternative to going to detention.

To make a long and happy story short, that young man got rid of his tattoo, got some decent clothes and a haircut, and continued on with school while working for Happy Joe's. He pulled down a 3.2 grade point average from that time on and eventually went into the auto body shop business where he found his niche.

Whitty-ism

Everyone has a spark in them. Help cultivate that spark in everyone you touch and you make the world a better place.

Family Members Working in the Business

I've always wanted my grandkids and my kids to work for Happy Joe's, but I also wanted them to work for other companies as well.

I don't think children can understand how different businesses operate until they have actually worked for them, and I also don't think they can see how unique Happy Joe's is until they have spent time elsewhere.

I've got a grandson named Anthony who has traveled with me since he was about three years old. No matter where I was–opening stores, doing promotional work, riding around in the fire truck or the tractor–all those years he was always right by my side. When he got older and started high school, and he was driving the fire truck and tractor and moving bales of hay and putting hay in the barns. Anything Grandpa needed to do, Anthony was there and willing to do whatever was needed. He also worked for Happy Joe's in all areas of the restaurant, both making and delivering pizzas. My grandson was following in the footsteps of all nine of my children–they all worked at Happy Joe's–and

Anthony learned the value of hard work and effort from the time he was a small child as well.

If you are starting a company and you plan to have your children work for you in order to hopefully have them take over one day, make them excited about working for your company. Pay them fairly. Treat them the same as the other individuals you have working for you—so that they can understand how hard work pays dividends in the long run.

I always wanted all my children to work at Happy Joe's forever and to ultimately be in charge of the company so I could go off and enjoy my retirement. But that's not how it happened. You can never plan for your children's own personality traits, and you should never force your children to have a career that doesn't make them happy.

I learned this lesson. It took me a little while, but it was a good lesson for me to learn.

My children are all so different.

My oldest, Larry, is everything I am not. Everything, for Larry, has to be in perfect shape. Even when he was a child, his room was always just so, and everything was all neatly lined up. He was never the outgoing center of attention that I had to be. Larry takes everything in, studies it carefully, and then makes his decisions and choices calmly and rationally.

My son Tim and I are the most alike. People just love him, and he can bluff his way through anything. He got my love of people and all my social skills.

Julie is the most like her mom. She is so sensitive and so intelligent. Her feelings bruised easily as a child, and she is just super smart. Julie always tries to make everyone feel comfortable and always thinks about everyone else and their feelings before she thinks about herself.

Kristel is a mix of both Sandie and me.. She has my people skills and love of talking and her mom's intelligence and sensitivity. Kristel is blessed with an amazing voice and is a wonderful performer.

Happy Joe's needed all four of my children's personalities. My children ended up being a good mixture that worked well together.

But eventually, when I sat back and looked at my company, I knew what kind of personality was needed to run it. I made so many mistakes by liking and trusting outsiders too much when I should not have. By the time I was ready to pass Happy Joe's along to my children, it was so big that I knew it needed someone who could work extremely hard going over business systems, strategies, figures, procedures, costs, and labor values all day long. I knew it needed Larry.

I wish I'd had Larry working for me at a management level when I opened my first Happy Joe's, because I know he would have kept me from making some really bad decisions. But since he was still in elementary school at the time, I thought I would give him a few more years.

I'm glad my children were able to reach out and decide for themselves what their dreams were, even if I would have liked for their dreams to be running Happy Joe's together. But that's not how it worked out.

Julie started the Happy Joe's human resources department and ran it wonderfully for years. Looking back now, I think maybe I was too tough on her because she was my daughter and I expected her to love what she was doing, even when I knew she wanted something else. Julie had always wanted to work in a place where she could help people. Finally, after having worked at Happy Joe's for over a decade, married with three kids, Julie decided she was going to make her dream come true. She decided to go back to school— not an easy choice with three little ones—to become an occupational therapist. She worked so hard to graduate, and she now has the professional career she dreamed about.

Tim didn't really like being tied down. He liked to set his own schedule—he was a lot like me. As Happy Joe's continued to grow, we didn't always see eye to eye. So he eventually decided to sell his shares in the company and do something he really wanted to do. Right now Tim is selling real estate and owns a property maintenance business. He has always been an extremely hard worker, and now he has work he loves.

And then there was Kristel. For a while there I thought she was going to be a permanent student. She went to acting school and singing school and was in a band with a tour bus. I had visions there for a while of retiring and just being her tour bus driver as she performed all over the country. But then Kristel ended up getting her MBA and decided Happy Joe's was where she really wanted to be. As marketing director for the entire franchise, Kristel doesn't get to sing as much as I would like her to, but she does an amazing job of keeping Happy Joe's fun and exciting and upbeat.

My kids are all facilitating my ease into retirement and are now running Happy Joe's. I show up in the office every once and a while to make sure my pictures are still hanging in the office, and they still are. I still have the biggest office with the best view, and I still put in about forty hours a week or more, but this time it's doing things I want to do, and I have a great time doing it!

Whitty-ism

Your family will always be your biggest asset, but they may also have different dreams than you. You can't force someone you love to be happy doing something they don't want to do; you gotta let them live their dreams also, even it's not the dream you want them to have.

Our Core Values

....

*W*henever anyone comes up with a new business, they've got to have a vision for their business before they even look over their first loan application. They have got to decide what the purpose of their business will be—what they want people to associate with their name.

I knew early on what the vision of Happy Joe's would be, because the name says it all: *Happy* Joe's. So our vision statement is simple yet says it all:

"Happy Joe's will exceed its guests' expectations in a manner that creates word of mouth praise, which will propel us into infinite success."

And then there's our core values. Decision making here at Happy Joe's is always done within the framework of what we call our core values.

Fun

Happy Joe's encourages an atmosphere for all team members and guests to enjoy their experiences.

Examples of our pursuit of this are things like our birthday parties, making a big deal out of our guests and their experience when they come in, and taking kids back to the kitchen to see how everything is made.

Fairness

Each of us makes every effort to treat people as we would want to be treated.

We shouldn't treat everyone equally as each of us has different needs, wants and expectations. But we certainly can treat everyone fairly. It just means "do the right thing."

Quality Image

Everything we do shall be done in the spirit of excellence. What we do will be done to portray the highest standards to our guests and team members regarding products, people, service, and atmosphere.

An example is our diligence in tending to such details as picking up cigarette butts in the parking lot, welcoming guests when they walk in, and stressing to everyone on the Happy Joe's team that if they got time to lean, they got time to clean! That means if they have the time to lean on the counter or up against the wall, then they have time to grab a rag and clean something up or make something inside the restaurant sparkle a bit more.

Balance

Happy Joe's promotes an environment that is sensitive to both the personal and career goals of our team members.

Examples are such things as our encouraging people to work smarter rather than necessarily harder. And we encourage the involvement of our team members' spouses. We have a scholarship program for our team members who want to continue their education and always strive to make allowances for family situations!

Community Involvement

Happy Joe's is committed to participating in local communities.

I talk about this throughout the entire book. Any business in any community has a responsibility to give back to that community. We are not alone in this world—and we all have something to share.

Risk Taking

Happy Joe's encourages managed risk-taking. We want our people to think outside the box to create new areas of guest satisfaction, product ideas, and operational systems.

We encourage all our team members to be active participants in new marketing campaigns, community ideas, and even new pizza creations! We love new and innovative ideas. I still remember being told in my much younger days by various companies I worked for that "We don't do that," whenever I came up with ideas to help sales or the community support. I encourage everyone to take that risk—you'd be surprised what comes from it! And if you decide not to take a risk, you've also made a risky decision, because you will then never know what could have happened.

Whitty-ism

Before you take the first step in starting a new business, decide what your vision will be and what your core values will be. You need to make sure you know what is most important to you before you can begin selling it to someone else.

Taco Pizza for All!

*I*t seems like every pizza joint nowadays has its own version of a taco pizza. It's fairly common to see that type of pizza listed in the menus of almost every major pizza chain today, especially here in the Midwest. But it never used to be that way.

I can state with confidence that Happy Joe's was the first pizza restaurant to offer taco pizza.

It all began in late 1974, when one of my franchisees asked me if he could begin serving tacos in his restaurant.

I loved eating tacos but thought that first and foremost we were a pizza restaurant. So I told him I thought it was a great idea but to let me play with it a bit and see if I could come up with something better than tacos.

I had no idea what I was going to do since I talked him out of tacos. I was sitting around thinking and then headed to the local grocery store to pick up a few taco makings. I went to one of my then two Davenport, Iowa, Happy Joe's locations, the one on Locust St., and started making pizzas. I made a taco pizza with taco meat and sauce. I didn't think it looked very pretty, so I played with it some more, adding my secret taco seasoning mix and cheese. It looked kind of nice, but it still didn't trip my trigger. So I added chopped lettuce and tomatoes and thought it was starting to look pretty good but still needed something. Then I thought about some specially seasoned taco chips.

So I went and got a bag and crushed up the chips and added them to the top of the pizza. The three employees working in the store at the time all tasted it and thought it was great. They then told me not to change it, because they all knew how I liked to tinker with food to make it better, and they said they thought it was just about perfect.

I had some good friends come on by and do a taste test. I also took one home to the kids. At first the kids weren't too excited about the new creation, because it was like nothing they had ever seen or heard of, but when I insisted, they tried it and absolutely loved it.

It took me all of two days to come up with the taco pizza, although I sometimes tell people it took me a lot longer than that.

The next step was convincing the franchisees to put it on their menu, which they were skeptical of doing. So I first put it on my company location menus, and people started talking about it.

That's when the formerly reluctant franchisees started calling me directly, asking when they could also start making and selling taco pizzas. So one of my employees would go to the stores and teach them how to make it. In about two years, every store was selling taco pizza—which is our number one seller today with a cult-like following.

When I ask people what kind of pizza they like the best, most say taco pizza. Our original pizzas we create on our own, like the taco pizza, are a big part of our sales success. The taco pizza is the first thing people recognize when new stores are opened. I guess it must be a compliment to see our competitors try to replicate their version of a taco pizza and then to hear our guests comment that, "No one makes a taco pizza like Happy Joe's."

Taco Joe

I learned that it does take a while for the consumers to catch on to a new product when you do not have a robust advertising budget and are left with product sampling and word of mouth promotion. Our franchisees were skeptical and reluctant to try taco pizza but now would not give it up.

Taco pizza was so popular, I knew I wasn't going to be the only place in town selling it for long, but I was pretty sure I was the first one, which, as far as I was concerned, made mine the best. Of course, it helped that all of our guests agreed with me.

It was sometime in September 1979, three years after Happy Joe's introduced taco pizza, that a Dallas, Texas, based pizza chain, Pizza Inn, put its taco pizza on the market, got trademarks on it in eight states, including Texas, and applied for a national trademark.

In the meantime, Pizza Hut had made its own version of taco pizza and began using the same name in its menus and advertising. Immediately, Pizza Inn sent a letter to Pizza Hut saying they owned the name. In a letter to the United States patent and trademark office, Pizza Hut claimed taco pizza was only a description like spaghetti, lasagna, or salad bar that could not be copyrighted and if Pizza Inn was granted the exclusive term of "taco pizza," it would have a virtual monopoly in the pizza business.

The Pizza Hut/Pizza Inn trademark battle spurred Happy Joe's attorney, Robert Van Vooren, sprung into action, and he fired off a letter to our patent attorney telling him to immediately file a resistance to the Pizza Inn application to trademark the name "taco pizza," because Happy Joe's had been selling the product since 1976, and had menus to prove it.

Pizza Hut came back with a letter to the patent attorney requesting confirmation of the name that Happy Joe's used when they offered their taco pizza product in 1976.

By now it was October, and our patent attorney wrote a letter to us explaining that he had written a letter to Pizza Hut and enclosed copies of the 1976 menus from Happy Joe's. In the letter the patent attorney indicated that Pizza Inn had obtained registration for "taco pizza" in Texas, but that such registration did not necessarily mean that Happy Joe's could not use the term and that we could contest the registration, if need be. Our patent attorney also indicated that he believed the term "taco pizza" was a descriptive term and that it would most likely never obtain federal registration. In the event it did obtain registration, our patent attorney assured Happy Joe's that he would immediately file an opposition to it.

At the same time the patent attorney wrote a letter to Pizza Hut explaining that Happy Joe's shared Pizza Hut's belief that "taco pizza" is a descriptive term and that it opposed Pizza Inn's attempt to register it as a trademark. He enclosed letters and menus that contained the use of "taco pizza" and stated that Happy Joe's would be willing to help however it could in the suit against Pizza Inn.

On December 5, 1979, Happy Joe's submitted an application for trademark registration of the name "Taco Joe" for its taco pizza.

On October 13, 1980, Robert Van Vooren received a letter from the patent and trademark office rejecting the request to trademark the term "taco," because it is a descriptive term.

And later on, Van Vooren received a letter from the patent attorney saying that he checked with Pizza

Hut, Inc., and that Pizza Inn had agreed not to assert any rights to the term "taco pizza." The patent attorney reiterated that none of the U.S. applications to register the term were successful, and that it is incapable of being a trademark.

So there I had it: I had worked hard at something and made something so popular that it was considered a household name in the United States. I got to admit, I was a little bit flattered, even if no one knew I was the first one to make a taco pizza. Unless they read my book.

Whitty-ism

Copying and imitation can be the most sincere forms of flattery…and be mindful of what can be trademarked! Also if you do not have a large advertising budget, be prepared to be patient as it will take a large effort with tiny results over a few years to create success with a new product.

Life Lessons

· ·

Business Practices and Marketing Strategies

Selling New Pizzas

There are important lessons I have learned in this section of the book and some new marketing ideas I came up with over the years to increase my exposure in the community and sell people on new ideas and concepts I came up with.

These are often not the sort of things that a person would learn in a formal class on how to market a company. They are more of a "fly by the seat of the pants" or "on the job training" kinds of things, but they have worked well for us here at Happy Joe's.

These techniques are illustrated and trained by storytelling here in our company to perpetuate our culture, since we have never been big enough to turn up the volume of advertising like our national competitors.

For example, back when I was more active in the day-to-day operations of our store or stores, I'd often see a construction job near the store.

If I was trying to find a market for a new pizza, I would give it away, bringing entire pizzas to construction workers. Later, I could almost always count on seeing those same workers stopping by my store for lunch or dinner.

I remember when I first developed Canadian bacon and sauerkraut pizza. I was in visiting some friends and family in Minot, and they decided they wanted the pizza guy to make homemade pizzas. So I whipped up some dough and let it rise to create what I thought would be the perfect crust. Then I found some sauce in the pantry, and went on a treasure hunt for toppings. I realized then I had forgotten to go to the grocery store, and would have to make do with whatever they had leftover in the house. I discovered some sliced breakfast Canadian bacon in the refrigerator, and a can of sauerkraut in the pantry and Bingo! Canadian Bacon and Sauerkraut Pizza was born, known today as the Happy Joe's Special.

When people first heard the name, many were absolutely not interested. So to get people interested in this unique pizza, I would carry some around with me and offer workers a free lunch. People didn't think much of it when I first brought it to them, but when I came back it would be all gone.

It is still one of our top sellers, and I'm surprised by how many of the young people enjoy it and say that even though they hate sauerkraut, they love our Happy Joe's Canadian bacon and sauerkraut. We continue to create new pizzas all the time. We want to keep things different. We started a couple of new pizza doughs recently that are multigrain and gluten-free. We continue to use high quality toppings for our pizzas. There will always be a cheaper product down the street, but that's not going to cause me to make a cheap pizza. We are going to continue to make our pizzas the way they are supposed to be made with abundant quality toppings.

Speaking of the sauerkraut pizza, I had a friend ask me a couple of years ago to come up to Milwaukee and speak at this sauerkraut convention. I was kind of tickled, so Nancy and I got all packed and headed up there. When we got to the hotel, they had a nice little room waiting for us, and I said I thought this was a pretty nice deal. I spoke at the convention for a while about how I came up with the idea of putting sauerkraut on pizza and added of a lot of jokes to my speech, and the audience seemed pretty amused by me.

The next morning, while still at the convention, Nancy asked me to get her some coffee. So I threw on a pair of sweat pants and headed downstairs.

I was all the way on the sixth floor, and when I got on the elevator, it stopped on the fourth floor, and three young, good-looking guys got on and they said, "How you doing, old timer?"

I remember thinking that no one had ever called me an old timer before, and it kind of burnt my tail, so I started kind of pouting in my corner of the elevator. Well, then the elevator stopped on the next floor, and three of the most gorgeous ladies I had ever seen got on, and I recognized them from the conference the day before.

They looked over, right past the young men, recognized me, and said very loudly but with a ton of enthusiasm, "Joe, you were terrific last night!"

These three young men looked at me, and they were still staring at me when they got off the elevator. I decided to not confuse the issue with explanations.

Whitty-ism

Sometimes the odd gets the attention...but only if promoted!

Fire Trucks

When a business of any kind first opens, you have got to let potential customers know about your existence before anyone will patronize your store.

Well, when we first opened I had no money in the bank, because I had spent my entire SBA loan just to get Happy Joe's up and running. I was basically open for business and just about broke; I didn't have money to spend on radio or television or newspaper advertisements.

I had to think of some way of promoting Happy Joe's to the customers of Davenport. Well, about this time the city had a big asset sale, and they had a beautiful old, antique fire truck up for auction. I thought if I could just get a hold of that thing I could put Happy Joe's on the side and make it look real cute and just use it for the parades and drive it around so everyone knew who we were. I thought that would be a really big deal.

So I went to the sale, and I was looking at this nice fire truck, and I started it up, and I listened to it run. I knew I wanted it, but I also knew I didn't have a lot of money to spend on it, so I was really hoping no one else was interested in it. I was willing to go up $5,000 on the truck but knew I couldn't afford much more. I figured, as a working fire truck, it was going to go for a heck of a lot more than I had to spend, but I figured it was a shot. When the auction started, I ended up buying the fire truck for sixteen hundred dollars!

So I painted the Happy Joe's logo on this fire truck and also wrote, "Follow this fire truck; it stops at all the Happy Joe's." I drove it in all of our community parades, and it was probably the best promotional piece I could have ever done. We also had a little fire truck one kid could ride in, and I had my sons Larry and Tim driving that in the parades. It was just a nice little promotional piece; we called it the "Little Joe."

Tim Whitty on the mini-fire truck

There probably isn't a kid alive who isn't excited about fire trucks. When we'd park our fire truck out in the parking lot, more than one car would suddenly slow down and stop in the parking lot. Kids would spill out, oohing and aahing over the sight of the fire truck.

And of course the chance for a ride on a fire truck was just about more than a kid could handle without swooning in delight.

Back in the days when we had but the one store, we'd tell the kids that that fire truck would make the rounds, stopping at each and every Happy Joe's. That seemed to impress them, even when they were aware of the fact that we had but the one store. That fire truck got us a lot more bang for the buck than traditional advertising ever could have.

Happy the Dog gets a ride on the
original Happy Joe's fire truck

Whitty-ism

Don't be afraid to think outside the box when coming up with ways to advertise your business, something catchy is always memorable!

The Sneaky Long Way Around

Another little trick I learned was that when a pizza would be delivered to a table or booth, the people that the waitress would walk past to get to the customer would get a whiff and a sight of that pizza and remark at how good that smelled and looked.

My little trick was to have the waitress take as long a route to the destination of that pizza as possible so as to pass by as many other tables and booths as possible.

I'll have to admit that the idea occurred to me to have that route wander on past the tables and booths in neighboring restaurants, but I never did go to that extreme.

One of the best things I ever learned was to pay close attention to what people were saying and their body language.

I learned, for example, that a few Catholic nuns would enjoy having a beer now and then with a meal, just like lots of other people. I also learned that the nuns would be uncomfortable by the odd looks they would get from other customers when they would see the nuns with a beer in front of them.

It didn't take long for me to come up with the idea of serving beer in paper cups when the customer was a nun. Apparently, people who saw a nun eating with a paper cup in front of her thought that she certainly had to be drinking something no more powerful than a soft drink.

When serving beer in paper cups, all it took was a little sly grin or a raised eyebrow to let them know we understood and were doing what it took to make them feel comfortable.

Whitty-ism

A little extra concern, care, attention, and service can go a long ways.

Ninety-Eight Years Young

There was an incident in which a ninety-eight-year-old fellow was in Happy Joe's for his birthday party.

I made a big deal out of all that by stopping by the man's table and announcing that the fellow could stop by for a birthday party twice a year instead of only once. I told the grinning birthday boy that the cost for the meal would be ninety-eight cents, with the price going up one cent every year. I also told him that I didn't want any complaining about the price.

NOT YOUR AVERAGE JOE

That "birthday boy" story got told and retold so often that lots of people knew how we had made a birthday pretty special for a ninety-eight-year-old kid.

Later on, when that gentleman turned one hundred, he told me with a twinkle in his eye that he wasn't going to be able to come for lunch anymore, because his meals would now be one dollar and that was just getting a little steep.

Whitty-ism

Never neglect an opportunity to make someone feel special. Personally, I've always loved the saying by Mother Theresa: "Let no one ever come to you without leaving better."

Let's Picket Happy Joe's!

I like the idea of making lemonade when you are handed a lemon. I also like to think that is exactly what I did one time when we found ourselves picketed for hiring electricians that had come in with a lower bid, unaware that they were not of union status.

I never did understand the union issues with my experiences. I was a businessman, and I was helping other businessmen start businesses. None of us were extremely wealthy, and our bank loans were always for minimum amounts. If we had a chance to save money, we were gonna take it!

199

But there they were, picketers, walking up and down the sidewalk in front of my restaurant, picketing our store, handing out fliers, urging people not to eat at Happy Joe's.

My son, Tim, was working at that particular Happy Joe's that afternoon, and he called me for advice on how to handle things. Well, an idea suddenly came to me on how to make lemonade out of this lemon.

I had Tim put up a message up on the marquee saying, "Bring in your fliers and receive two dollars off your next pizza." There, in just a heartbeat, the guys passing out those fliers were actually passing out coupons for two bucks off on lots and lots of pizzas.

Those fellows on the picket line simply laughed at me at first. Then they got a bit confused when they realized they were encouraging and supporting people to eat at Happy Joe's. People were stopping by the picketers, asking for a flyer, and then promptly walking in my restaurant to eat lunch or dinner.

It wasn't long before they held some whispered conversations and then went home. I guess they got tired of promoting Happy Joe's for free, but I really appreciated their support.

Whitty-ism

Making lemonade out of life's lemons can actually be a lot of fun!

The Booster Seat Incident

One evening a family came into my new Happy Joe's restaurant. They had heard about the excellent pizza and unique ice cream creations, so they decided to come and check Happy Joe's out. The family consisted of a mom, a dad, and two children. One of the children was a toddler about two or three years old. The family came in, and I immediately showed them to the best table in the restaurant. As they took their seats, I noticed the mom was holding her toddler on her lap.

I said to the mother, "Would you like the little one to have his own chair?"

The mom said, "Oh, I think those chairs are still too big for him yet. He is a little too big for a high chair and a little too small for a normal chair, so I usually just hold him on my lap when we go out."

"Well, that's okay," I said, "but what about a booster seat?"

"A booster seat? What's that? I have never heard of one."

"Hold on just a minute," I said. "I'll go get one to show you."

In just a few seconds, I came back with a booster seat. I pulled out a chair and placed the booster seat on it. I then looked at the mother and reached out my arms to the little boy. "May I pick him up?" I asked.

"Yes."

I then picked up the little boy, placed him in the booster seat, and pushed his chair against the table. The little boy got quite a smile on his face and immediately looked at his mom as if to say, "Look at me. I'm in a big-boy chair!"

"Oh, for heaven's sake," the mother replied. "Isn't that a wonderful invention?

"And it's so simple," the father chimed in.

The little boy's older brother said, "It looks like he likes it too!"

The family thanked me and proceeded to order their meal.

I checked back with the family periodically throughout the dinner. The family had a large pizza, and they were just finishing up their ice cream when I made one last stop at their table.

"Well, folks, was everything okay tonight?"

"Oh, it was all wonderful,"

"This is the first restaurant we have been to in a while where Mom didn't have to eat with my brother Matt on her lap."

"So he liked the booster seat?"

"Oh, yes," said the mother. "He felt like a real big boy having his own chair just like all of us."

"Well, I'll tell you what. I want Matt to take this booster seat home with him tonight so he can be a big boy at the supper table at home too."

"Oh, no, Joe. We can't take your booster seat."

"No, I want Matt to have it," I said. "Just promise you will come back every once in a while so I can see how big these kids are getting and serve them up some pizza and ice cream."

"Are you sure?" the dad asked.

"I insist. Take home the booster seat and enjoy it!"

The family thanked me again several times and left the restaurant with the booster seat.

Now, back in 1972, believe it or not, booster seats were a new thing. They had just come out for restaurants, and they were not cheap. I had just started my business, and I had invested all of the money I had into it. Frankly, I really wasn't in a financial position to give away my new, expensive booster seats for free, but I was always a good risk-taker, and I believed that every once in a while you had to give a little more than you think you can afford, and you'd get a whole lot more back later. Well, it turns out that in this case I was right.

That young couple with those little kids not only came back regularly, but they brought in other families as well, who told and retold the booster seat story time and time again over the years.

I would hear people say, "Hi, Joe. We're friends of the family you gave the booster seat to. We've heard so much about you and this place from them that we just had to come and see it for ourselves."

It turns out this family was quite connected in the community, and they had been passing out that story of the booster seat to nearly everyone they knew. They sent tons of business to Happy Joe's and were there themselves regularly afterward. This family is still coming to Happy Joe's today, and they are still telling the story of how they first met me and all about the booster seat. With all of the business they have brought to Happy Joe's over the years, we could have purchased thousands of booster seats.

This story continues to be used as a training example to Happy Joe's team members. We encourage all new hires to invoke the notion of good deeds to create positive moments and words of praise throughout their communities.

Whitty-ism

Never miss an opportunity to do something small for someone that could lead to something much bigger, and use it in "storytelling" to your new hires for them to understand your desired culture of taking care of people!

Estate Site Selection

After I'd been in business for several decades and had multiple Happy Joe's franchises around the Midwest, I got invited to speak to a bunch of university students on restaurant management. I was sort of edgy over the whole thing, seeing as I never had that high degree of education, and then got even more nervous when I listened to a whole clutch of experts whose talks came before mine.

These fellows had all sorts of impressive degrees and credentials they apparently found it important to talk about. They were polished and professional speakers who knew all about restaurant management.

One of the things those fellows all touched on was the importance of location. They had all kinds of fancy (and expensive) ways of figuring out where to locate restaurants. They pretty much dazzled us with exotic and complicated mathematical formulas on how to select sites for restaurants. I know it impressed me, and I figured the students must have been wowed about all that too.

By the time it was my turn to talk, I felt like the country boy from Des Lacs, North Dakota, that I was, and I felt a bit over my head.

I went through with it, hoping I didn't sound too much like a country bumpkin.

Then one of the students raised his hand with a question, "How does Happy Joe's choose a location?"

Well, you can bet I didn't have any fancy engineering models or mathematical formula to lay on the questioner, so I just looked at him, looked at the rest of my audience, shrugged, and told them truth: "I just look for a Wendy's, McDonald's, or some other popular chain somewhere nearby. They spend a lot of money on research for locations. And then I open next to them."

Judging from how the audience reacted to that, I have the distinct impression that those kids learned a lot about how to site a restaurant from that Des Lacs country boy that day.

Whitty-ism

Degrees are nice. Being smart is even better.

Mud Flap

*S*everal years ago at the Happy Joe's home office, the president of the company, Larry Whitty (my son), arrived at work early one Monday morning. And as he pulled into the home office parking lot, lying in the area near where all of the office staff usually parked their cars was a large object. Larry parked his car and walked over to the object to see what it was. It was a big mud flap that had obviously fallen off some large truck or semi.

Larry bent over to pick up the mud flap with the intention of throwing it away, but then he had a thought, *I wonder if any of our office staff will notice this big mud flap lying here as they pull into our parking lot for work today. Surely they will see it. It's very hard to miss. It's a huge, white mud flap lying on our black pavement. They have to notice it, don't they? This is a definite eyesore. It's a big piece of garbage.*

So Larry decided not to throw away the mud flap and to see what would happen as the office staff came into work.

Larry went into the building and awaited the arrival of his employees as he watched through the window to see what happened. It wasn't but a few moments before the first car pulled into the parking lot. The office staff member parked his car, grabbed his briefcase, and proceeded into the building without pausing to notice the mud flap. Needless to say, Larry was disappointed.

Soon after, more cars pulled into the office. Staff members parked their cars and walked into the building together, chatting without noticing the mud flap. Then the next car came into the office lot and parked, and the occupant began walking into the building.

She was headed right for the mud flap, and Larry thought, *Okay, here we go. She has to notice it. It is right in front of her.*

The staff member veered slightly to avoid the mud flap as she entered the building. This went on until all of the office staff had arrived at work, and none of them appeared to notice anything about this big ugly mud flap that was lying in plain sight as they all entered the building.

On Monday mornings at the Happy Joe's Support Center, the staff gets together for a weekly meeting. The agenda usually consists of President Larry going over all of the projects and plans for the week. All of the office staff filters into the conference room where these meetings are held.

Larry excused himself for a moment while everyone was getting settled. In a few moments, he came back into the room carrying the mud flap and took his place at the head of the table. He laid that mud flap in the middle of the table. Of course, now everyone in the room noticed it, but they were not really sure why it was there or what Larry was up to.

"Does this look familiar to anyone?" Larry asked.

The group looked at one another trying to figure out whose mud flap this might be. Everyone was clearly "clueless" as to where Larry was going with this.

Larry continued, "This mud flap was in our parking lot this morning. I was going to throw it away but decided to leave it where it was to see if any of you would notice it and take it upon yourselves to dispose of it. Not one of you appeared to notice it. In fact, one of you even went out of your way to walk around it! If this had been laying in your front yard at home, I have a good feeling you'd have noticed it very quickly and would have gotten rid of it immediately.

"Why do you think no one addressed it here at work? Don't you care about our work environment? Don't you want to work at a place where things are nicely kept? Why didn't you notice this?"

The group was clearly dumbfounded. They had no good answers for Larry's questions, and they realized they had disappointed him by not noticing the mud flap.

Larry was not angry with the group. He knew that it was probably not intentional that the mud flap did not get noticed, but he was concerned about the lack of observation his staff exhibited that day.

"How many other mud flaps are there in our restaurants that we could be missing or walking over every day?"

When Larry used the term "mud flaps," he meant it as an analogy, meaning how many other things are going on at our restaurants right in front of us that we are not seeing?

"Are we walking over garbage and cigarette butts as we walk into our restaurants and not addressing them? Are we not noticing things like crooked pictures on the wall or the fact that we have a light bulb out in the restaurant? What if our marquee was missing some letters? Would we notice?"

Today when the word "mud flap" comes up in a Happy Joe's conversation, everyone knows it isn't a real mud flap being talked about. It's a problem that someone should have noticed and fixed even if it wasn't his or her job.

What if a guest is unhappy or a team member is not well groomed or the garbage can is overflowing? Would these things catch our eye?

The group now clearly understood what Larry meant. We have to work together as a team if we want to have a well-run company with well-run restaurants. It doesn't matter whether it is your job or not. We all work together. Imagine that this is your restaurant. Wouldn't you want your team to care about how it looked and what kind of reputation it had?

Whitty-ism

Watch out for mud flaps, and find similar examples to use in "storytelling" for your culture!

Drawing the Line

I think when someone has pride in their accomplishments it's fairly easy to pass that pride along to someone else. I think when we treat others as well as we treat ourselves, the world becomes a better place all together. On the flip side, it's fairly easy for any of us to understand that a company that shows little or no concern for the welfare of its employees is a company that is going to end up paying dearly for that.

It certainly isn't in a company's interest to have its employees mad at it and for them to be always on the lookout for some way to get even.

Not only are there practical reasons to be a boss who cares and to be a company that cares; it's just plain wrong not to be concerned about the well being of the people in your employ. It doesn't take a whole lot of smarts or a big ego to realize both the moral and the business imperatives to treating people right.

But there is another side to that. It can be destructive to the company and to people's lives to put them in a position where they can take advantage of concern and decency and to leave such an individual in a position of power in your company.

I'll have to admit that it has been more difficult for me to draw the line between proper concern for employees, associates, suppliers, etc. and going too far in being "Mr. Nice Guy." Many times in the Happy Joe's experience, I have leaned over too far in an effort to see to the good in people.

Occasionally this has come back to bite me and to bite the company.

It took longer than it should have for me to understand that if a particular person and Happy Joe's is a poor fit, then it doesn't do anybody any good to try to salvage a relationship between that person and the company.

I have looked past conduct that was not good for an individual or for Happy Joe's and given someone a fourth or fifth chance. Too often when I should have cut a final paycheck and escorted a transgressor to the door, I've given them "one more chance."

One of the most destructive things you can have running loose in the company is a person who knows he's on the way out but has two weeks, or whatever time, to work all kinds of mischief.

We've had situations like that, one of which ended up costing us hundreds of thousands of dollars. In that particular case it wasn't an employee involved but a store owner. The slack I cut that fellow gave him time to do a lot of real mischief.

I had hired a man to manage Happy Joe's franchises. We both got off on the wrong foot–his hours didn't fit with mine, mostly because he was unavailable when I needed to talk to him. And I found myself needing to talk to him a lot, because the man was constantly cutting down on serving portions and purchasing product from unauthorized companies with unacceptable quality standards.

That is not the Happy Joe's image franchisees agree to support when they open a restaurant, and I wanted this practice halted immediately.

Then I discovered this man had added terms to a franchise contract without my knowledge. The first time he did this, I found out later, was when a franchise location he had once had an interest in changed hands. He put a stipulation in the contract that said no one else could open a Happy Joe's within a greater-mile radius of this store than our typical standard.

So when we unsuspectingly opened a new store, the owners of the franchised store threatened to sue me, and I was completely bewildered as to why…until I saw the contract they had signed. A contract with provisions in it I had never seen nor added. Before all was said and done, it cost Happy Joe's hundreds of thousands, a very expensive lesson.

Another time my son Larry was attending college in Denver, so I called him one day and asked him to drive to Idaho to see how a store up there was doing, because I was having a lot of trouble making contact with the owner, which my manager also had an interest in. When Larry got there, he found a closed sign on the door. The owner had just shut it down without telling me.

Once again, "nice Joe" got taken. Instead of firing that man on the spot, I gave him two weeks to find another job. But during that time period, instead of looking for a job, he spent time conducting more unethical business practices that cost Happy Joe's even more money.

I've always believed that the best way to run a company is to do what is right. But it isn't right to enable and host a person to do wrong.

Again, I like to think that I have been a caring employer and Happy Joe's has been a caring company. I've always been aware of the usefulness of that quality. It just seems that there comes a time to end a relationship–and to end it quickly.

Not only does ending a relationship that isn't working in the best interest of the company, but it can also serve the best interest of the individual.

Yet in spite of the costs and the reversals, the tears and the disappointments–that sense of caring has been a cornerstone upon which Happy Joe's has been built. I am willing to accept the occasional costs of caring when the positive results of that so often bubble to the surface and spread out around me.

Hiring has two critical mistakes that should be avoided that most of us seem to make:

1. Recognize you have hired the wrong person.

2. Terminate the relationship sooner rather than later.

Robert Lewis, our training director, best described this situation as: "There are no bad employers, and there are no bad team members–but at times there can be a bad fit.

Whitty-ism

Getting a non-working relationship behind us provides a reason for the individual to look around to find where he does fit in.

Reflections

$\mathcal{I}$ think about my Grandpa Shaffer living with us on the farm all those years. It's not like that anymore. Today when a grandpa gets too old to take care of himself, he gets shipped off to the nursing home. Things have changed.

I think money changes everything, especially people. Still, I would hope that money has not changed me. I was just as happy as a kid, working for pennies an hour, as I am now. Money bought me material things, but it hasn't made me any happier than when I bought that Model A and got it running.

I think happiness can come from a lot of things but not necessarily from money. I think you need to find what makes you happy and just do it, even if other people around keep muttering it can't be done. I'm seventy-five years old and have been through some tough times, some tragic times, and some wonderful times, but at all times I try to live up to my name. I try to be Happy Joe. Besides, they say happy people live longer, and I'd like to be around to see Happy Joe's hit their fiftieth, sixtieth, and what the heck, seventieth anniversaries.

I've tried to base my life by following my dad's example: be generous, always be good to everybody, and be willing to help people. I grew up thinking, *That's the way to do things.* Helping others is the best feeling of all. When you help somebody, you walk away feeling good.

I remember one time a neighbor had a heart attack. My dad said, "You're going over there and milking his cows."

All I could think was that was a heckuva lot of work to do. But that neighbor put me on a pedestal of sorts when he got out of the hospital and told people what a good guy I was because I worked for nothing. All of a sudden, I got a feeling that that type of encouragement was better than getting paid.

When I was ten years old, my dad had a health problem and had to go to the hospital. My brother, Tom, and I said we thought we could handle things at the farm, but we were extremely overwhelmed by all the work ahead of us. Then that Sunday morning, we looked up the road, and about thirty tractors were coming our way. They called it a "farming bee." They came to put in the crops and cut the hay and were finished by four that afternoon.

Grandpa stood at the end of the line and passed out cold beer each time a tractor passed him. He also thought it was a good idea to have one himself. Somebody forgot to tell him he was not supposed to have a beer *every* time a tractor came by.

Remember where you come from. Grandma
and Grandpa Whitty on their farm.

My mother butchered a bunch of chickens and made
a big feed for the guys. We called the gas company, and
the truck came out and filled all the farmers' tractors
before they went home. I began to realize these people
are the kind who are helping people all the time, but
you never get to read about them or hear about them.
There's a lot of those people out there—ones who do
nice things over and over and not for credit or to get
their names in the paper. They do it because it's the
right thing to do.

I believe that time is a valuable thing to give to
people. Money is nice, but time can fix a problem forever.

When I was a kid, it was a chore working on the
farm, but now it's fun. I will spend all day mowing the
lawn. Of course, I don't think anyone can mow better
than I can. I like to make it pretty. I was fussy when I
plowed on the farm. I would drop the plow in the same
spot every time. I enjoy sitting on the tractor. It's a great
place to think. Years ago I must have married fifteen

different girls in my mind while riding on the tractor. I always was thinking about what kind of life I would have when I got older.

Now I think about my kids and grandkids. How are they gonna do? And I think about my age. I'm getting close to the ninth inning. How will I handle that? What kind of situation will I be in? I hate to think the ball game is close to over, because it's been such a great game.

I think about not being a burden to my family. Nobody wants to be a burden to others.

I see generosity and fairness in all my kids, and it makes me very proud. I'm sure their mom sees this from where she is. I'm happy that nothing evil has messed up their minds—no cheating and no dishonesty. People who work at Happy Joe's know that if something bad happens to them, we will be there in a minute to help out. One time there was a fire, and one of our employee's houses burned down. It wasn't five minutes until we had money together and made sure that his family was assisted. And we didn't need a meeting to decide.

One day someone asked me if I owned a newspaper. I was set back a bit and said, "Do I own a newspaper?" He said, "Yeah, you're in the newspaper a lot."

It's too bad that when you do something good for someone it becomes news. We all should be doing it all the time, and then it would not be news.

I was used to working sixty to seventy hours a week in a bakery. When the kids were growing up, I needed to work to pay the bills. I learned real quickly—the harder you work, the more money you make. There is always someone who says, "You were really lucky! You hit it at the right time." I don't know if it was luck or being smart–probably a little of both.

Sometimes I think it would be fun to dump everything, walk away, and start all over again. Seeing something start from nothing and making it something is a big thrill. I'm itching to open a bakery. I probably should never have sold my bakery in the village. That bakery was a haven for me. I like to put my hands on things. Baking bread is fun. You open the oven door, and there are fifty loaves of bread all proofed up beautiful. That's a high for me. Twenty minutes later you open the oven door, and there sits an angel food cake. I get twenty-five or thirty highs a day from baking.

I don't work sixty or seventy hours anymore, but I come down to the office, work a while, and then go home and work on the farm the rest of the day. I don't call that work anymore.

When I left the farm, I said, "I don't ever want to see a farm again."

Now I'm sitting at the kitchen table, and I see a board loose on the fence, and I can hear my dad saying, "Are you gonna look at it, or are you gonna fix it?"

All of a sudden I'm hobbling out on my bad leg and hammering on the fence. While I'm out there, I'm thinking, *A fence that needs fixing won't let go 'til it gets fixed. An oven full of loaves of bread won't be happy until those loaves are all baked and sliced, and kids aren't "done" 'til they are properly raised.*

I determined that the demands life places on us are never-quittin'.

Heck, while I'm fixing that fence, I might as well paint the board. The board next to it doesn't look so good either, so all of a sudden I'm painting the whole darned fence.

Yeah, sometimes I realize I'm never-quittin' like those winds that scour the prairies of North Dakota.